MW01014331

GEEK SWEETS:
an adventurer's guide to
BAKING WIZARDRY

60+ recipes to level up your baking game!

JENNY BURGESSE

For permission requests, please contact the publisher at:
Mango Publishing Group
2850 Douglas Road, 3rd Floor
Coral Gables, FL 33134 USA
info@mango.bz

For special orders, quantity sales, course adoptions and corporate sales, please email the publisher at sales@mango.bz. For trade and wholesale sales, please contact Ingram Publisher Services at customer.service@ingramcontent.com or +1.800.509.4887.

Geek Sweets: An Adventurer's Guide to the World of Baking Wizardry

Library of Congress Cataloging
ISBN: (print) 978-1-63353-616-6, (ebook) 978-1-63353-615-9
Library of Congress Control Number: 2017915763
BISAC category code: CKB004000, COOKING / Methods / Baking

Printed in the United States of America

Disclaimer

To **my friends**, who offered both their support and to eat the leftover buttercream, to **my family**, for the love, the tried & true recipes and the countless trips to the farmer's market with a full trunk, and to **Mr. B**, who I can't wait to grow old and gross with, after a long, amazing adventure.

CONTENTS

FOREWORD BY JEN YATES OF *CAKE WRECKS*

I have a theory that baking is actually *magic*.

Think about it: It requires a rudimentary knowledge of potions, it casts a spell over everyone who smells, sees, or eats it; and most suspicious of all, *bakers almost never wear pointy wizard hats.* Why is that, if not to throw us off the scent?

If you've picked up this book, then odds are you like baking. And magic. And kittens wearing tiny hats, because who *doesn't* like kittens in tiny hats? **People who won't like this book, that's who.**

(Just to be clear, there aren't any kittens in tiny hats in this book [OR ARE THERE?], but there *is* unicorn poop, which is surprisingly more tasty.)

(Also to be clear, I haven't eaten any kittens in tiny hats to compare their taste to unicorn poop, and it's weird I have to clarify that.)

Maybe I should start again.

The first time I met Jenny was at a signing party for my book *Cake Wrecks*. She fed my entire audience of Canadians crap-shaped cupcakes, and *they loved it.* So much so, there was very nearly The Politest Scuffle In The World over the last cupcake. So when I heard Jenny was writing this book, I knew two things: 1) that it would hit the sweet spot in the Venn diagram of all things tasty, adorable, and delightfully geeky, and 2) there would probably be poop in it.

I was right, and that's why you're going to love this book. Because you need your baking to be a little more *fun*. A little more weird. A little more YOU.

So whether you're into gaming or fantasy or explaining how Han made the Kessel Run in 12 parsecs, get ready to embark on the tastiest quest ever. Because hey, when it comes to baking? It's dangerous to go alone. **Take this book.**

(I mean, go pay for it first. I am NOT advocating shoplifting. *That would be a terrible foreword.* It's bad enough I've said "poop" this many times.)

(I said "poop" again. *Crap.* I mean *shoot.* Sorry. I'll stop now.)

- **Jen Yates**, author of *Cake Wrecks: When Professional Cakes Go Hilariously Wrong*

DUNGEON MASTER'S PREFACE: USING THIS BOOK

How to turn your baking trials into critical hits.

I've been waiting for you, adventurer.

Here in this darkened corner of this forsaken tavern, where I've been spending my days telling stories to anyone who'll listen of baking adventures past. But the further away those days of baking wizardry get, the more hazy the accounts become. I mean, I barely even tweet anymore.

But I awoke with a start one night not too long ago, and I just *knew* this book had made it to your hands. I sensed you were coming; your eager mind and limitless baking potential was like a pulse of brilliant light from that haze of darkness.

And how did you come across this tome, adventurer? Perhaps you discovered it in the forbidden section of a Mage tower library, or journeyed up a mountain to be handed a copy by a withered shaman, eager to pass on his mystic baking arts. Or maybe you bought it off Amazon. However it ended up in your hands, its power is now yours to wield.

Before you venture far from the comfort of your starter area, we should discuss the items below for an overall understanding of how this book works and the journey that now lies before you.

Levelling Up

This book is divided into 3 parts, each increasing in difficulty. Always read the recipe all the way through before starting! Get familiar with the steps before you take them, and it will improve your baking experience.

If you are new to baking, I recommend starting at Level 1 and working your way up. If your baking skills are already maxed out, then feel free to jump in and start slaying dragons all willy-nilly.

Level 1 - Squire: Starter quests to begin your baking adventure.
Level 2 - Knight: Grinding your skills in the kitchen for maximum XP.
Level 3 - Dragon Slayer: Epic recipes and skill checks for the most heroic of bakers.

The final section of the book is titled Festival Reveler, and it will be your chance to do a victory lap. Celebrate the seasons with a glass of mead and these legendary seasonal recipes.

Side Quests

Every adventurer needs a little break now and then. Between each level, there are recipes to help you plan a sweet shindig for your adventuring party (and some new NPCs you may meet along the way). A printable party invite, recipe, and cocktail are included for each theme party to get the festivities started.

Essential Baking Spells

Pages 42 to 75 contain the essential baking spells required to make most of the recipes in this book. Learn them well, adventurer, and they will serve you in kind.

Templates

Included in many of the recipes are names of templates available for download from my website, books.geeksweets.net – they are used for cutting out specific shapes, usually for fondant or cookies, as well as for royal icing transfers. See page 206 for how to use templates with fondant, page 35 for how to use templates with cookies, and page 128 for how to use templates to make a royal icing transfer. If you don't have a printer, use this quick tip: trace template shapes by holding a square of waxed paper up to your computer screen, tracing the shapes, then cutting them out as required.

Download and print templates

Fondant template in use

Cookie template in use

Royal Icing template in use

Critical Misses

Keep in mind this eternal truth: there is no winning or losing when it comes to baking. Each creation is a step on your journey toward true baking wizardry. If something doesn't come out the way you imagined or looking just like the photo, it's all the same to your taste buds, bud. Pick yourself up, dust the cake crumbs off, and try again.

Rolling Natural 20's

Just pulled off a feat of baking prowess the likes of which this realm has never seen? I'd love to see it! Share it with everyone on social media with the hashtag #geeksweets and I'll share it too:

Twitter: @geeksweettweets, Instagram: @geeksweets, Snapchat: @geeksweetsnaps
Facebook: @geeksweets

We've been talking all night, and the sun is starting to crest on a new day. Time to go, adventurer, our quest begins. These old bones can still conjure a mystical sweet or two. Let's settle up with the barmaid and leave this small town behind for the buttercream-frosted glory that awaits.

ADVENTURER'S INVENTORY

Leveling up your baking game with an arsenal of goodies.

Clear up some slots in your Bag of Holding – baking magics require the right tools for every spell. You will find details in alphabetical order below on many of the items you'll need to recreate the recipes in this book, as well as swap-in suggestions for some harder to find items.

Not sure where to find something? Check the resources section of this book, on page 259, for places to purchase the inventory items not yet in your armory.

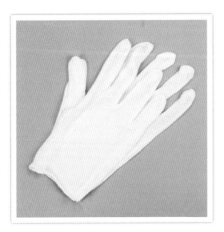

Chocolate Handling Gloves

Yep – these are a thing. They're thin, cotton gloves that keep fingerprints off your chocolate creations when picking them up. They can be purchased online or from bakery supply stores, and they are great for handling chocolate coming out of silicone molds or for adding chocolate toppers to cupcakes without leaving any trace of yer grubby paws.

Cookie Lifter

These small, flat spatulas are great for – you guessed it – lifting cookies on and off a cookie sheet. Always wait until your cookies have cooled two or three minutes before sliding this puppy underneath them and moving them to a cooling rack, otherwise they will be too soft and prone to breaking. If you don't have a lifter, wait until cookies are completely cooled before lifting them off the cookie sheet with a gentle twist.

Couplers

These are used to hold small piping tips in place in a piping bag. (More on tips later!) The two brands I use most frequently are Wilton and Ateco. But be careful – the Ateco couplers and tips do not "play nice" with the Wilton couplers and tips, so be sure to use tips with the matching brand of coupler. See page 27 for details on how to put together a piping bag with a tip and coupler.

Cupcake Baking Pans

These are usually called "Muffin Tins", but let's not fool ourselves - we know what we're using them for. Use a standard size, and make sure they're not marked "Jumbo". Mini sized tins can be used for making miniature versions of all the recipes in this book, but baking times will be shorter – keep an eye out for golden tops and check the centers for doneness with a toothpick. Also keep in mind, dark colored pans cook their contents faster, and lighter pans cook them slower.

Cupcake Corer

This fun little gizmo will make light work of popping the middle out of a cupcake in order to add filling. While it sure is nifty, a thin paring knife will also do the job. Cut a hole two-thirds of the way down into the cupcake and tilt knife upwards to remove the 'cake plug.' Be careful not to cut the hole too wide – try and cut it the way you would cut the top off a Halloween pumpkin, keeping uncut cake on all sides

Cupcake Liners

These are available in a variety of colors, from simple white to a jazzy rainbow leopard print number. Any color can be used with any cupcakes; however, color and style recommendations are made with most of all the cupcake recipes in this book.

Disher / Ice Cream Scoop

While both can be used to dole out an equal amount of cake batter into a cupcake pan, color-coded scoops called "dishers" are used for portion control in food preparation and restaurants and can take less trial-and-error than finding the perfect ice cream scoop. My go-tos are a #20 yellow disher for portioning my cupcake batter, and a #40 purple for portioning cake pops. I also use the #20 disher to help determine how much frosting to dye / flavor for a particular number of cupcakes, at one scoop per cupcake.

Edible Ink Pens

Like food dye, but in a handy felt-tip pen applicator. A few companies make them, but by a wide margin, Americolor pens are the best quality and last the longest, and they work on a wide variety of surfaces. Edible ink pens are great for details on cake pops and fondant, or anywhere you need a quick, small application of color. While they come in all colors, I find I use the black 90% of the time, so keep that one in good supply. The black can be purchased in a pack of two on their own online, or in a pack with all the other colors.

Flavoring Oils

When lemon zest alone just won't cut it, these oils extend your flavor possibilities. Need your cupcakes to taste like cotton candy? No problem! There's a flavoring oil for that. Add slowly and to taste, keeping in mind that the baking process will remove some of the flavor. That being said, try not to go overboard! I use an eyedropper to add the flavoring from these small vials, ensuring that I don't just upend the bottle accidentally and put someone into a Cotton Candy Coma™.

Fondant

Fondant is like the modelling clay of the baking world. It is made out of sugar and water, with gelatin and glycerol to make it stretchy and malleable. You can dye it, flavor it, shape it, spread it out thin to cover frosted cakes, and dry it to cut shapes out of it with an X-acto or sharp paring knife. My brand of choice is Wilton, as it dries at a decent speed for cupcake toppers when thin, stays moist enough for shaping when thick, and is dry enough that it doesn't stick to your fingers like crazy.

Fondant Glue

This simple "glue" is made at home, and is used to stick things to fondant, or to stick fondant to itself. Take a one-inch ball of fondant, and put it in a small, shallow microwavable dish with a teaspoon of water. Microwave on high for about 20 seconds, or longer if required. Stir mixture to create glue texture, adding more drops of water if needed. If glue starts to thicken back up while in use, add a few more drops of water and microwave again until it is the desired consistency.

Gel Food Coloring vs Liquid Food Coloring

There is a big difference between these two types of food coloring. While the liquid coloring you can buy in a grocery store is good for coloring other liquids, they will not do the trick for buttercream or batter as the dye is not concentrated enough. Gel dyes can be purchased online or at specialty baking / crafting stores like Michaels or Bulk Barn. In contrast to liquid dyes, only a tiny amount should be used, and it can be doled out using a toothpick. Be careful not to "double-dip" as that can transfer bacteria to the tub of dye. They last almost forever, but always keep a lid on them, as they will dry out to a rubbery consistency if left open to the air.

Luster/Disco Dust

Luster dust is an edible dust that adds a shimmer to your baked goods, while disco dust is a coarser edible glitter that can be used in the same way. They can be watered down into a paintable paste with a few drops of vodka, or dusted dry on a surface with a large, soft paintbrush. Luster dust can also come in a spray can, which is useful for spraying a metallic sheen onto something wet, like the top of a frosted cupcake. A 24k gold dust can even be purchased and used in very small amounts for an *extremely* metallic effect.

Paint Brushes

Two paintbrushes should be purchased and used for only food-related purposes: A small detail brush to paint on watered-down dusts and dyes (among other fancy things), and a large fluffy brush to pick up and dust on edible glitter or brush luster dust over large areas. Always wash and dry well after each use.

Piping Bags

I recommend investing in a good quality plastic-lined cloth or silicone piping bag that will hold your large cupcake frosting tips. These bags can be rinsed out with soapy water and easily reused over and over. They have to be kept clean and dried out well after each use to avoid retaining any smells or discoloration.

I also recommend having a stock of disposable plastic bags for small quantities of royal icing or for recipes where you will need multiple colors at once and may not have many reusable piping bags. These are also handy for melting candy melts in the microwave. These disposable bags can also be rinsed out and reused to prolong their lives, but they won't last forever.

Piping Tips

While there are a vast array of different piping tips out there, here are a few specifics that top my list – you'll see them used throughout this book:

For decorating cupcakes: Ateco 845 (large star tip) and Ateco 809 and 806 (large round tip) will cover almost every type of frosting technique in this book.

For decorating cookies: Ateco or Wilton in a size 1 for the tiniest details, size 5 for covering large areas, and size 3 for just about everything else. I have about 15 of these tips for cookie decorating that requires a lot of colors.

Ateco and Wilton brand tips are the most popular and can be purchased online or in baking supply stores like Michaels or Bulk Barn.

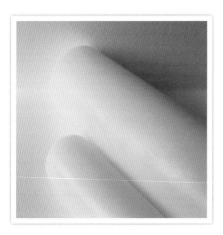

Rolling Pins and Rings

While rolling pins come in many varieties, my favorite is the Wilton 20" Fondant Roller. It's huge, it's smooth, it's easy to clean and it packs a mean wallop should an army of orcs invade while you're prepping your cookie dough. I also like the smaller 9" roller when rolling out small amounts of fondant - though a round, clean pen or pencil will also do the trick!

Spatula

Several good spatulas will serve you well for many baking tasks. From scraping the bottom of a mixer bowl to incorporating all the dry ingredients to scooping buttercream into a piping bag, you'll always have a use for a good spatula. I recommend the silicone variety as they are flexible and easy to clean.

Sprinkles

While sprinkles come in a wide variety of shapes and sizes, the ones you'll use most in this book are as follows:

Jimmies – Long thin sprinkles in a rainbow of colors *(Figure 1)*,

Confetti – Round flat circles, usually sold in a mixed color variety *(Figure 2)*.

Nonpareils or Dragées – Teeny, tiny balls in varied sizes, usually in rainbow colors or coated in metallic gold or silver *(Figure 3)*.

Sanding Sugar – Coarse grain sugar, great for adding a bit of sparkle and crunch. *(Figure 4)*.

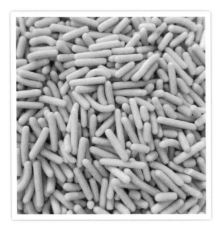

(Figure 1)

(Figure 2)

(Figure 3)

(Figure 4)

Stand / Hand Mixer

I have (and worship!) a shiny silver KitchenAid mixer; I call it "The Silver Surfer." While I recommend a stand mixer for anyone getting into baking in a serious way, all recipes in this book can also be made with a handheld mixer. In fact, some recipes, like the 7-Minute Floofy Frosting on page 66, will specifically require a hand mixer. I would recommend against hand mixing the recipes in this book with a spoon, no matter how buff your biceps are, particularly the Buttercream frostings, which require a large amount of air to be incorporated.

Vanilla Bean Paste vs Liquid Vanilla Extract

While there's no doubt that liquid vanilla from the baking aisle of your local grocery will do the trick, there's nothing quite like the professional presentation provided by vanilla bean paste. While both vanillas will taste very similar in your recipe, the tiny black flecks reminiscent of a scraped vanilla bean pod that appear in your cake or frosting are a visual reminder of the vanilla flavor dancing on people's taste buds. You'd be surprised how much of a boost the extra sensory cue adds to the cake 'nomming' experience!

Whisk

Often, recipes will have you sift your flour with a sifter. This is to separate any clumps and make it easier to combine it with other dry ingredients, as well as with the wet ingredients. The same effect can be achieved with a metal whisk and some vigorous stirring, and using a whisk will save you having to keep a sifter around the kitchen. It can kick up a mean flour dust cloud, however, so maybe do your whisking near the sink.

Wooden Toothpicks

Between using toothpicks as cake testers and scooping up bits of gel dye with them, I go through a crazy amount of toothpicks. To check that your cupcake or cake is baked through, stick a toothpick into the very middle, right down to the bottom. If the toothpick comes out clean, then your batter is baked through. If not, it needs to go back in the oven for a few more minutes. Don't be deceived! Make sure it's batter you're seeing on the toothpick and not a sneaky melted chocolate chip.

X-acto Knife

I like keeping some of these sharp blades on hand to cut around templates in both fondant and dough. Be sure to use them on a cutting board, and don't chop up your kitchen counter. A thin, sharp paring knife can also be used instead. Either way, be careful around the pointy end, adventurer. #sharpthingsaresharp

SKILLS TRAINING AND COMBAT TRICKS

Masterful baking comes from sweet foundations. And practice, practice, practice.

As a budding baking adventurer, you'll want to become proficient in a variety of skills that will aid you on your journey. Your charisma stat may be through the roof, but if your dexterity is lacking, you'll end up with more frosting on your tabard then on your cake. Today your training in the foundational skills required for the recipes outlined in this book begins. The trials ahead may be dark and full of terrors, but you'll be ready – let's get started.

(Figure 1)

How to Portion Out Buttercream

When portioning out how much buttercream you'll need to frost your cupcakes, it's a good idea to use an ice cream scoop or disher, with one scoop per cupcake *(Figure 1)*. If you only need 5 cupcakes with green mint frosting, put 5 scoops of your prepared buttercream in a separate bowl, then tint and flavor it before putting it in the piping bag. Then if you have any leftover buttercream, you can save it for later in the fridge, wrapped in a square of plastic wrap.

(Figure 2)

How to Fill a Piping Bag

Drop a piping tip (or a coupler, if you're using a small tip) into the bag. Using scissors, cut off the tip of the bag, removing only as much as it takes for the coupler / tip to *just* stick out of the bag *(Figure 2)*. If you cut it too wide, the opening will stretch under the pressure of piping and launch your piping tip across the room, along with a gob of buttercream frosting. Slide your large tip out until taut, or attach the small tip and outer ring of your coupler.

Hold the piping bag in your left hand around the middle, and fold the edge over your hand. Using your right hand, fill the bag with frosting using a spatula *(Figure 3)*. You can use the edge of your left hand to wipe the frosting off the spatula. Do not overfill! Fill the bag just over halfway and no more, or you won't be able to twist it shut without it oozing out of the back of the bag.

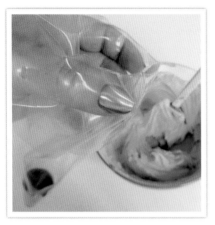

(Figure 3)

(Figure 4)

Twist the bag closed until all of the air is pushed out of the bag and the frosting comes peeking out of the tip. You're ready to go!

How to Frost a Cupcake

Now that you've got your piping bag full of buttercream frosting ready to go, let's get to piping! Different tips have different effects, depending on the type of frosted cupcake you're looking to make, but almost all of them require the same motion – rotating at the wrists.

A common error I see when people are learning to frost a cupcake is that they move their upper arms and hands in small circles over the cupcake, like they're stirring a pot. Instead, make sure you are rotating *only your wrists*, and in circles that, with each rotation, grow smaller. Usually it takes about two and a half rotations to get there. When you reach the center of the cupcake, release pressure and pull up quickly for a pointed tip. This gives you much more control over your movements and keeps you centered over the cupcake. Watch someone making ice cream cones from a soft-serve machine – it's the same movement, just upside down!

It may help (or hinder!) to pick up your cupcake in your other hand while you pipe, as opposed to keeping it on a flat surface. Give both methods a try and see which you prefer.

Pictured are some of the different frosting effects that can be achieved and the tips used to create them:

✦ *Classic Rosette:*

This technique is common for a reason – it's super easy! The ridges fall however they feel like falling and hide any imperfections, air bubbles, or required restarts.

Starting at the outside edge of the cupcake and rotating at the wrist, make two and a half rotations, making each one smaller to create a dome. Release pressure and pull up once you reach the center of the cupcake.

Tip: Ateco 845 or Wilton 1M

✦ *Flat Rosette:*

This is your classic "I'm going to jam a bunch of stuff on top of this cupcake so it can't be super tall" frosting technique. It also looks very pretty on its own!

Starting at the center of the cupcake and rotating at the wrist, make two and a half rotations, making each one larger until you reach the edge. Release pressure and wipe the last bit of frosting around the outside edge so it blends in.

Tip: Ateco 845 or Wilton 1M

✦ *Princess Rosette:*

This ruffle-icious technique uses a star tip with more prongs to create a shape much like a bridesmaids' dress from the 80's. I won't lie, adventurer – getting the hang of this one takes some practice, so test it out on some waxed paper first, then scoop the testers back into your frosting bowl once you've got it down. Make one rotation around the edge of the cupcake, then make a bunch of tighter circles, quickly and closer to the center, letting the ruffles fall as they may.

Tip: Ateco 849

✦ *Flat Top:*

This is like a Classic Rosette, but with less height and a large round tip. Great for cupcakes where you will be dipping the tops in sprinkles, graham cracker crumbs, or melted chocolate.

Starting at the outside edge of the cupcake and rotating at the wrist, make two and a half rotations, making each one smaller to create a dome. Press down harder and do not lift up as much as you would with a classic rosette. Once you *almost-but-not-quite* reach the center of the cupcake, release pressure, and instead of pulling up, continue rotating and blend the tip of the frosting with the rest so it sits flat.

Tip: Ateco 809

✦ *Tall Coil:*

This uses the same technique as the Classic Rosette, but with a smaller round tip. It's not recommended you use this style for chocolate frosting, lest the coil resemble… well… poop (unless that's the effect you're going for, like with our Poopcakes on page 120!) It also uses a smaller round tip than the Flat Top, as it would otherwise be an overwhelming amount of frosting. And that's coming from someone who's DTF: Down to Frost.

Starting at the outside edge of the cupcake and rotating at the wrist, make two and a half rotations, making each one smaller to create a dome. Release pressure and pull up once you reach the center of the cupcake.

Tip: Ateco 806

✦ *Grass:*

This one's self-explanatory, adventurer – frosting that looks like grass. S'right there in the name. This tip also makes great shaggy monster fur in a pinch!

Place tip in the middle of the cupcake touching the surface, and squeeze bag to form grass. Pull straight up while keeping steady pressure on the bag, and when strand is long enough (about one-third of an inch), release pressure and pull away quickly. Grass will be neatly formed only if you stop squeezing before you quickly pull the tip away.

Tip: Wilton 233

✦ *Multicolor Frosting:*

This takes some extra work to put together, but comes out quite impressive. You can keep it as simple as a two-color combo, or go up to five for a stunning rainbow effect, like the Rainbow Dash cupcake from the Cutie Mark Cupcakes recipe on page 176.

Fill up to five disposable piping bags with each different color of frosting. Do not fill them as full as you would a regular piping bag, as they will all need to fit back into one bag at the same time *(Figure 5)*. Cut the tips off each bag, and drop them all together into a piping bag fitted with a large star tip *(Figure 6)*. Twist the back ends all together and squeeze until you see all your colors coming out of the tip at once *(Figure 7)*.

Starting at the outside edge of the cupcake and rotating at the wrist, make two and a half rotations, making each one smaller to create a dome. Release pressure and pull up once you reach the center of the cupcake *(Figure 8)*.

Tip: This works with any tip as long as it's large, but an Ateco 845 or Wilton 1M has the best effect for a ruffled star shape, or use an Ateco 806 for a round coil.

(Figure 5)

(Figure 6)

(Figure 7)

(Figure 8)

Frosting Troubleshooting

I can't even squeeze it out of the bag!

If you find that your frosting is very hard to pipe, it may be too cold. It should be at room temperature when frosting, and so should your cupcakes, so they don't just melt their frosting right off.

Nope, it's room temperature and it's still not coming out.

If the frosting is too thick, it will be difficult to pipe and may even break when you attempt to pipe it in a curve. Pop it back into the mixing bowl, add in some milk (or liquid non-dairy creamer or coconut oil for the vegan Butterless Buttercream), and mix until it has a silkier texture, fit for piping. Usually the longer you whip your frosting, the easier it will be to pipe.

No sprinkles are sticking to it!

Buttercream may develop a crust on top as it sits, which will make the sprinkles just bounce off like arrows off that sweet new armor you just equipped. Make sure to sprinkle early and sprinkle often! If you miss your sprinkling window, give your frosted cupcake a quick spritz of water from a spray bottle set to the 'fine mist' setting, and you'll be back in business.

How to Dye Fondant

While fondant can be purchased in a variety of colors, I find it's easier to take white fondant and dye it as required.

Only use gel dye to dye fondant, and always wear gloves when you do, as the dye is very hard to get off your hands. Protect the table you are working on with a piece of waxed paper, and never set dyed fondant down directly on any surface you don't want dyed.

Gloves worn should be plastic and not latex, as latex will stick to the fondant and drive you bananas. If you can't find gloves, you can also pop your hands inside two plastic or ziplock bags and handle the fondant that way.

Add dye to fondant using a toothpick, a little bit at a time *(Figure 9)*. Be careful – you can always add more dye, but you can't remove any once it's mixed in. Fold the fondant over on itself, sandwiching the gel dye inside, and stretch, then fold again *(Figure 10)*. Repeat until all dye is incorporated and color is even.

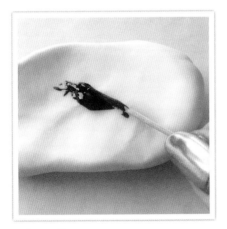

(Figure 9)

(Figure 10)

How to Roll Out Cookie Dough Like a Boss

Step up your cookie rolling game with the following rolling technique:

Take freshly mixed dough and place a big blob between two sheets of waxed paper.

Roll it out to the desired thickness (usually one-third to one-quarter of an inch) *(Figure 11)*. Place the "rolled dough and waxed paper sandwich" you've just made on an upside down cookie sheet and pop it into the refrigerator *(Figure 12)*.

(Figure 11)

(Figure 12)

Continue rolling out your dough between sheets of waxed paper and adding it to the pile on the back of the cookie sheet until you have used up all the dough. By the time you are finished, the first sheet of dough will be completely chilled and ready to cut *(Figure 13)*.

Cut cookies shapes with a cookie cutter or use a printed Geek Sweets template *(Figure 14)*.

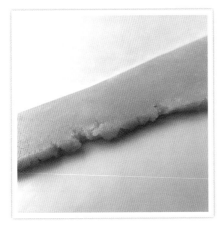

(Figure 13)   (Figure 14)

Here's why rolling out your cookies this way rocks – they're easier to lift and put on the cookie sheet when the dough is chilled through, and you don't end up incorporating additional flour into your dough, which can make your cookies dry and tough. Not to mention your kitchen won't look like you were on the losing end of a messy bout with some vengeful spirits.

How to Cut Cookie Shapes Using a Geek Sweets Template

Visit books.geeksweets.net to download the specific template mentioned in the recipe. Print at 100% and cut out cookie shapes along dotted lines. Place template onto cookie dough surface and cut around edge using an X-acto knife or a sharp paring knife *(Figure 15)*. The template will get greasy as you go along, but will hold together. You can store templates in a ziplock bag for future use if desired.

Use the waxed paper under the dough to help you lift intricate shapes onto a cookie sheet. *(Figure 16)*.

Chill and reroll leftover dough, and repeat the process until you're all out of dough.

(Figure 15)

(Figure 16)

How to Dam and Flood a Cookie

Almost all cookie decorating starts with this one crucial step, which will ensure that your frosting stays where you want it to. Royal icing oozes like lava, slow but unstoppable, but the Dam and Flood technique will keep it in its place.

First, make sure your cookies are completely cooled! No piping onto toasty warm cookies. Fit a piping bag with a #3 Ateco or Wilton tip, and fill with prepared royal icing. Prepare a second bag filled with the same color with a #5 tip. Make sure to cover any remaining icing with a wet paper towel or cloth so it doesn't dry out.

Pick a spot and begin piping an outline of icing onto the cookie with the #3 tip *(Figure 17)*. Your icing should flow in a solid line from the piping tip and not break. If it's breaking, it is likely too thick. This creates a border or "dam" so the 'fill' icing does not flow over the edges *(Figure 18)*.

After allowing the dam to dry for a minute or two, fill the middle of the cookie with the same color frosting from the bag fitted with the #5 tip (Figure 19). The reason for the larger tip is so it is easier to fill quickly. At this point, I like to pick up the cookie and give it a little wiggle to get it to settle nice and flat *(Figure 20)*.

(Figure 17)

(Figure 18)

(Figure 19)

(Figure 20)

Keep a toothpick handy to pop any air bubbles or help push frosting into any intricate corners of your cookie shape *(Figures 21 and 22).*

(Figure 21)   (Figure 22)

Allow to dry completely before adding any additional frosting elements. (Or else don't, if you need to press anything into the wet frosting, as you do with the Melted Snowman Cookies on page 246.)

SKILL CHECK:

When piping cookies, you will get a straighter line if you hold the tip about half an inch to an inch away from the surface of the cookie, and let the icing string 'fall' into place. The closer your tip gets to your cookie, the shakier your line will be. Try it on a piece of waxed paper until you get the hang of it. (Don't try to scrape the testers back into the bowl, however, as they will be too dry and will cause your frosting to have lumps that will get stuck in your tip.)

How to Use Luster Dust

Luster dust can be painted onto just about anything to provide a little drama. It's completely edible and completely *faaaaabulous*.

To paint onto chocolate or fondant: Luster dust will stick much better to both chocolate or fondant with a little condensation. Put the chocolate or fondant pieces in the fridge to chill for 5-10 minutes, then bring back to room temperature. Condensation will soon start to form, and when it does, get dusting with a large, soft brush *(Figure 23).* For even quicker condensation formation, wave your fondant piece or chocolate *very quickly* over the steam from a kettle (being very careful not to scald yourself)!

To paint small details: For a little gold button or any other equally tiny detail, mix luster dust with a few drops of vodka or other alcohol and paint it on with a tiny details paintbrush *(Figure 24).* Alcohol will evaporate, leaving the concentrated luster dust behind.

(Figure 23)

(Figure 24)

— ESSENTIAL —

BAKING SPELLS

"The basic recipes from which legendary delights are conjured."

Many of the creations in this book refer back to these tried and true basic recipes as their starting point. The secret behind Geek Sweets' wide variety of flavors when selling at farmer's markets was being able to take a single vanilla cupcake recipe and create four or five different varieties of cupcakes using different flavorings, colorings, fillings, and techniques.

These basic recipes will be your greatest ally on your journey toward baking wizardry. Learn them well, adventurer!

QUEST REQUIREMENTS:

1 box white cake mix

1 cup all-purpose flour

1 cup granulated sugar

¾ teaspoon salt

1 tablespoon baking powder

1 ¼ cups water

2 tablespoons vegetable oil

3 eggs

1 cup sour cream

1 teaspoon vanilla

Flavoring oil (as listed by the individual recipe)

Stand or hand mixer

Cupcake pan(s)

Cupcake liners
(color as recommended by the individual recipe)

SKILL CHECK:

For some festive flair, mix half a cup of rainbow sprinkles (the long, tube-like ones called jimmies) into the batter before baking. While you can use other types of sprinkles to make a "confetti cupcake", they are more likely to run – their rainbow-y goodness may smear into the batter and blend into more of a greyish mess.

FOOLPROOF VANILLA CUPCAKES

I know what you're thinking: "A cake mix!? That's cheating! Someone tell the DM!" Settle down, adventurer, and keep reading.

Below is a variation on a recipe very popular in internet baking circles, called 'White Almond Sour Cream Cake' (or 'WASC' to High Baking Wizards in the know). It bakes a cake that is consistent and sturdy, yet moist and light, making it ideal for stacked wedding cakes or anytime you need a trustworthy, foolproof recipe for a high-concept flight of baking fancy. It also takes well to added flavoring oils or mix-ins like nuts, citrus zests, and chocolate chips.

This recipe has been a constant companion throughout my baking adventures, and I hope it serves you just as well.

MAKES **22-25 CUPCAKES**

Preheat oven to 350° F and line cupcake tins with cupcake liners.

Add all dry ingredients to a large mixing bowl, or to bowl of stand mixer, and mix until combined. Add the remaining ingredients and beat on low speed until combined, scraping the sides and bottom of the bowl with a spatula as needed.

Using a large ice cream scoop or disher, fill cupcake liners two-thirds of the way full.

Bake 18 minutes, or until a wooden toothpick inserted into the center of the cupcake comes out clean. Carefully remove from the cupcake pan and allow to come to room temperature.

Cupcakes can be stored overnight at room temperature, or frozen up to two months in airtight containers to decorate at a later date.

¾ cup unsweetened cocoa powder

¾ cup hot water

3 cups all-purpose flour

1 teaspoon baking soda

1 teaspoon baking powder

1 teaspoon salt

1 ½ cups butter

2 ¼ cups granulated sugar

4 eggs

1 tablespoon vanilla

1 cup sour cream

Flavoring oil
(as listed by the individual recipe)

Stand or hand mixer

Cupcake pan(s)

Cupcake liners
(color as recommended by the
individual recipe)

SKILL CHECK:

These cupcakes rise up beautifully
with a big domed top, so be wary
of over filling your baking cups with
batter – two-thirds full is what you're
aiming for. If you want consistently
sized cupcakes every time, check
out the section on Dishers in the
Adventurer's Inventory at the
beginning of this book, (page 15.)

MOIST CHOCOLATE CUPCAKES

These cupcakes start out on the stove with melting the butter and sugar together before incorporating your other ingredients – a strange beginning compared to the well-worn "creaming of the butter and sugar" path we're used to. But I wouldn't lead you astray, adventurer. The road to rich chocolate cupcakes lies before you – and none are more worthy to traverse it.

MAKES **30-32 CUPCAKES**

Preheat oven to 350° F, and line cupcake tins with cupcake liners.

In a medium-sized bowl, whisk together cocoa and hot water until smooth. Then in a large bowl, mix in flour, baking soda, baking powder, and salt until combined.

Melt butter with sugar in a saucepan over medium-low heat, stirring to combine. Be careful not to let sugar burn!

Remove from heat and pour into a mixing bowl or the bowl of a stand mixer, then mix on low until cooled, about 6-7 minutes. Mixture must be cool enough that it won't cook the eggs you're about to add.

Speaking of eggs, add those to the melted butter and sugar mixture, one egg at a time, beating until each is incorporated and scraping down sides of bowl as needed. Add vanilla, then add cocoa mixture and beat until combined.

Add dry ingredients one cup at a time, mixing until combined.

Divide batter evenly among lined cups, filling each three-quarters full. Bake 15-20 minutes, or until a wooden toothpick inserted into the center of the cupcake comes out clean. Carefully remove from the cupcake pan and allow to come to room temperature.

Cupcakes can be stored overnight at room temperature, or frozen up to two months in airtight containers to decorate at a later date.

QUEST REQUIREMENTS:

½ cups granulated sugar

1 ½ cups vegetable oil

2 ½ cups cake flour
(not all-purpose)

2 tablespoons unsweetened
cocoa powder

1 teaspoon salt

2 large eggs

2 tablespoons red gel-paste
food color

1 teaspoon pure vanilla extract

1 cup buttermilk

1 ½ teaspoons baking soda

2 teaspoons white vinegar

Stand or hand mixer

Cupcake pan(s)

Cupcake liners
(color as recommended by the
individual recipe)

SKILL CHECK:

No cake flour? No problemo! You can approximate cake flour by adding two tablespoons of cornstarch per cup of all-purpose flour. But… why? Well, to get a real light and fluffy cake, you need light and fluffy flour with less protein, unlike with bread, where you want increased protein for chewy, glutenous goodness.

RED VELVET CUPCAKES

Red Velvet. All the most popular elves are talking about it, taking instagram "elfies" with slices of it, and wearing lip glosses flavored like it. But what is it, really, aside from the most popular cupcake in town?

It's moist, it's delicious, it's… red. And it has a distinct flavor all its own. Most red velvet recipes are oil-based, which gives them their soft texture; red velvet also has a slight tartness from the inclusion of buttermilk (or sometimes milk curdled with vinegar). Red velvet recipes also usually call for cake flour, which gives them a lighter crumb. But their greatest intrigue lies in the cocoa: with not so much as to venture into chocolate territory, yet not so little cocoa that it goes unnoticed, the flavor of red velvet rides the line between chocolate and vanilla, and falls into the literal sweet spot between the two.

MAKES **22-24 CUPCAKES**

Preheat oven to 350° F and line cupcake tin with cupcake liners.

Add cake flour, cocoa, and salt to a large mixing bowl and whisk until combined.

With a stand or hand mixer on medium-high speed, mix together sugar and oil until combined. Add eggs one at a time, beating until each is incorporated and scraping down sides of bowl as needed. Mix in food color and vanilla.

Reduce speed to low. Add flour mixture in three batches, alternating with two additions of buttermilk, and mixing well after each. Stir together the baking soda and vinegar in a small bowl. (Mixture will foam! Fun!) Add fizzy mixture to batter, and mix on medium speed 10-15 seconds.

Divide batter evenly among lined cups, filling each three-quarters full. Bake 20 minutes, or until a wooden toothpick inserted into the center of the cupcake comes out clean. Carefully remove from the cupcake pan and allow to come to room temperature.

Cupcakes can be stored overnight at room temperature, or frozen up to two months in airtight containers.

QUEST REQUIREMENTS:

1 ½ cups all-purpose flour

1 cup granulated sugar

¼ cup unsweetened cocoa powder

1 teaspoon baking soda

½ teaspoon salt

1/3 cup vegetable oil

1 teaspoon vanilla

1 teaspoon white vinegar

1 cup water

Flavoring oil (as listed by the individual recipe)

Stand or hand mixer

Cupcake pan(s)

Cupcake liners
(color as recommended by the individual recipe)

VEGAN CHOCOLATE CUPCAKES

For vegan adventurers! Pair with the Butterless Buttercream recipe on page 68.

MAKES **12 CUPCAKES**

Preheat oven to 350° F and line cupcake tins with cupcake liners.

Add all dry ingredients to a large mixing bowl, or to bowl of stand mixer, and mix until combined. Add the remaining ingredients and beat on low speed until combined, scraping the sides and bottom of the bowl with a spatula.

Using a large scoop or just a spoon, divide batter evenly among lined cups, filling each about three-quarters full.

Bake 18-20 minutes, or until a wooden toothpick inserted into the center of the cupcake comes out clean. Carefully remove from the cupcake pan and allow to come to room temperature.

Cupcakes can be stored overnight at room temperature, or frozen up to two months in airtight containers to decorate at a later date.

1 ¼ cups all-purpose flour

¾ cup granulated sugar

1 teaspoon baking soda

½ teaspoon salt

1/3 cup soy milk (or other non-dairy milk)

1/3 cup vegetable oil

2 tablespoons vinegar

2 teaspoons vanilla

Flavoring oil (as listed by the individual recipe)

Stand or hand mixer

Cupcake pan(s)

Cupcake liners (color as recommended by the individual recipe)

VEGAN VANILLA CUPCAKES

For vegan adventurers! Pair with the Butterless Buttercream recipe on page 68.

MAKES **12 CUPCAKES**

Preheat oven to 350° F and line cupcake tins with cupcake liners.

Add all dry ingredients to a large mixing bowl, or to bowl of stand mixer, and whisk until combined.

In a separate bowl, add remaining ingredients and mix until combined.

Add wet ingredients in with dry and beat on low speed until *just* combined, scraping the sides and bottom of the bowl with a spatula. Be careful not to overmix as this can lead to denser cupcakes.

Using a large scoop or just a spoon, divide batter evenly among lined cups, filling each about three-quarters full.

Bake 18-20 minutes, or until a wooden toothpick inserted into the center of the cupcake comes out clean. Carefully remove from the cupcake pan and allow to come to room temperature.

Cupcakes can be stored overnight at room temperature, or frozen up to two months in airtight containers to decorate at a later date.

1 box cake mix (any flavor or as directed per recipe)

1 container pre-made frosting (any flavor or as directed per recipe)

Flavoring oils (optional or as directed per recipe)

1 bag candy melts

9" x 13" cake pan

Waxed paper

Lollipop sticks

Plastic microwavable cup or bowl, deep enough for dipping

Toothpicks

Piece of styrofoam to hold pops as they dry

SKILL CHECK:

Some recipes in this book will have you "core" your cupcakes in order to add filling. You can save these cores in a plastic sandwich bag in the freezer to be added to your crumbled cake mixture once they've come to room temperature. Check page ** for instructions on how to core a cupcake using a cupcake corer or a knife.

CAKE POPS

Part chocolate, part cake, part lollipop, all delicious! First made popular by Angie Dudley of Bakerella.com, these adorable bites of cake on sticks have endless potential to showcase your creativity. If you're new to cake pops, don't be daunted by the large number of steps. All it takes is a little practice (and someone around who's willing to eat the duds)! Read on for the basics on how to put together the perfect pop.

MAKES **40-50 CAKE POPS**

Bake cake mix according to directions on box and let cool completely. (Don't skip this cooling step! The cake should be at room temperature before heading to the next step.)

Break up half of cake into pieces and place in food processor *(Figure 1)*. Blend briefly, until broken up into smaller pieces, then add in the other half of the cake and blend until cake is crumbled into small pieces *(Figure 2)*.

(Figure 1)   (Figure 2)

Add frosting to the crumbled cake one large spoonful at a time *(Figure 3)*. After each addition, blend in food processor in 10 second bursts until cake mixture begins to 'come together.' You'll know you've reached this stage when it reaches the consistency of Play-doh and starts to make a ball inside the processor *(Figure 4)*. Test a handful by rolling it into a ball – if it holds its shape, you're good to go!

This blending step can also be done by hand in a large bowl. It's harder, messier work this way, adventurer, but I know you're up to the task if need be.

(Figure 3)

(Figure 4)

Using a medium scoop levelled off with your thumb, dole out mixture into equal sized portions and place on waxed paper *(Figure 5)*. Shape into balls by rolling in your palms, or shape into whatever form the recipe you're following dictates *(Figure 6)*. (Roll into balls quickly after portioning, as the mixture will begin to dry out.)

(Figure 5)

(Figure 6)

Add one cup candy melts to a plastic, microwave-safe bowl or cup, and microwave in 30 second intervals until just melted, stirring after each interval. It should be warm, but not burning hot. The melted candy should be about three inches deep in order to fully submerge the cake pop. The thinner the coating, the easier it will be to dip the pop; so if you find the candy melt is not runny enough to drizzle off a spoon, melt a small amount of vegetable shortening into the mix to thin it out.

It's time to dip! One pop at a time, dip one-half inch of a lollipop stick into the melted candy melts, *(Figure 7),* then insert the lollipop stick into cake ball, pushing it in about half to two-thirds of the way through *(Figure 8).* (Don't let it pop out the other side!)

(Figure 7)   *(Figure 8)*

Allow candy melt to set before attempting to dip the pop – usually by the time you've attached all the sticks, the first ones you did should be ready to dip. If your bowl of candy melts has begun to harden on the edges, remelt in the microwave in 30 second bursts.

Holding the lollipop stick, submerge the entire cake pop into the candy melt until it creates a seal at the base of the pop *(Figure 9 and 10).* You want to accomplish complete submersion all in a single dip, or the weight of a "double-dip" will pull the pop right off the stick.

Once coated, gently tap the stick against the edge of the bowl / cup, while rotating the cake pop until all the excess candy melt has dripped off the pop *(Figure 11).* Place the cake pop into the styrofoam block to dry, stick side down. Be sure to set them far enough apart so that they don't bump into each other.

At this point, while the candy melt is on the pop but still wet, attach any elements required by the specific cake pop recipe *(Figure 12).* Do not draw on pops with edible ink pens until candy melts have dried completely.

(Figure 9)

(Figure 10)

(Figure 11)

(Figure 12)

Repeat with the remaining balls of cake mixture and let them completely dry in the styrofoam block before attaching any additional elements.

Store cake pops for up to one week in a cool, dry place.

Troubleshooting:

"I don't need 50 cake pops, that's too many cake pops!"

I get it, not every occasion calls for a full complement of 50 cake pops. If you want to make a smaller amount of cake pops, use half of the baked cake instead, and save the remaining cake un-crumbled in the freezer for a later date.

"My cake mixture won't hold its shape!"

You likely need more frosting in the mix to make it less crumbly. Aim for the texture of Play-doh when blending your cake pop mixture.

"My cake is falling off the stick when I dip it!"

Oh no! Don't worry, adventurer, it happens to even the most advanced warriors.

Possible causes are:

✦ Cake mixture was too crumbly – try adding more frosting until it's closer to the texture of Play-Doh.

✦ Cake mixture is too warm – working in a very warm environment? Try sticking the pops into the fridge for 30 minutes to an hour to firm them up slightly. But be careful – pops that are *too* cold can cause the coating to crack.

✦ You're tapping the candy coating off too furiously – use a gentle hand when tapping. You're tapping a cake pop, not wielding a mace, adventurer!

✦ The candy melt mixture is too thick – try thinning it out by melting in some vegetable shortening.

✦ Your cake pop is too big – the bigger the pop, the harder they fall. Keep your pops to a manageable size and they won't be too weighty for the stick.

The candy melt coating cracked!

This happens when the cake ball inside is too cold when dipped. I find just working with the pops in a cool room, without putting them in the fridge to firm up at all, gives me the least cracks.

The cake pop appears to be… oozing?

If your pop is starting to leave an oil trail similar to a runaway gelatinous blob, it's likely that you didn't completely seal the pop when you dipped it. Check the bottom and see if there is a gap where you can see the cake mixture, or if there is a small crack. You can fill in the gap with a small amount of melted candy melt on a toothpick.

SKILL CHECK:

*Buttercream icing will eventually
form a thin crust on its surface,
so any sprinkles should be added
immediately after frosting is piped
onto the cupcake – otherwise they
will just roll off the crusted surface.
I recommend frosting no more than
six cupcakes at a time before adding
sprinkles, chocolate chips,
coconut, etc.*

CLASSIC BUTTERCREAM

*Every adventurer should have their go-to 'weapon of
choice' when it comes to frosting, and this recipe is it.
Wield your piping bag with confidence – this versatile
recipe will let you frost your way out of any situation. It
can be easily flavored, colored, and piped in a variety of
styles and shapes. Check out the Frosting Techniques on
page 28 to see it in action.*

MAKES **5 CREAMY CUPS**

Beat butter with a mixer on medium-high speed until pale
and creamy, about two minutes. Make sure butter is at room
temperature before whipping. You can speed this process
by unwrapping it and placing it on a plate in the microwave,
then microwaving in 15 second bursts, rotating between
each burst, until just softened.

Reduce speed to low. Add sugar, half a cup at a time,
beating after each addition. Once all sugar is incorporated,
increase speed to medium-high and beat until fluffy, about
five minutes. (Don't skimp on the mixing! The longer you
whip the frosting, the more air is incorporated and the
fluffier and easier to pipe the resulting frosting.)

If you find the frosting is too thick, add milk, one
tablespoon at a time, stopping when it reaches a smooth
spreading consistency.

Add in gel food coloring with a toothpick as recommended
by the individual recipe and mix until combined. (Start slow –
you can always add additional color, but you can't remove it!)

Mix in vanilla or any flavoring oil as recommended by the
individual recipe.

Insert recommended tip into piping bag, and follow the
frosting techniques as illustrated on pages 27 - 33.

8 large egg whites

2 cups packed brown sugar

Pinch of salt

3 cups salted butter, room temperature, pre-whipped until light and fluffy

Stand mixer

Double boiler, or a mixer bowl set over a pan of simmering water

Piping bag

Piping tip (as listed in the individual recipe)

SKILL CHECK:

Icing may seem to curdle once butter is added. Fear not, adventurer! That's completely normal at this stage. Press on – continue to beat on medium-low speed, and the icing will come together with time into the smoothest, creamiest frosting you've ever eaten. There will be bubbles from all the whipping, but you can use a spatula to press the bubbles out against the side of the bowl before adding frosting to a piping bag.

BROWN SUGAR SWISS MERINGUE BUTTERCREAM

Take buttercream to the next level with this smooth, creamy, rich frosting. While it requires some strong magics to pull off, as well as some trickery over a bowl of simmering water, the result is a heady elixir that adds +10 AMAZING to any cupcake it tops.

MAKES **4 CUPS OF BUTTERCREAM BLISS**

Whip room temperature butter in stand or hand mixer until light and fluffy, about five minutes. Transfer to another bowl, then clean mixer bowl very well before next steps. You'll be using the bowl to whip egg whites, and any grease remaining in the bowl will stop them from coming together properly.

Whisk together egg whites, brown sugar, and salt in mixer bowl placed on top of a pan of simmering water on the stove. Cook, whisking constantly, until the sugar has dissolved and the mixture is warm to the touch (about seven minutes.)

You can tell the sugar is dissolved by putting a bit of the mixture between your fingers and rubbing it together to make sure there are no longer sugar granules.

Transfer mixer bowl back to stand mixer. Using the whisk attachment, beat on medium speed until fluffy and cooled, about 15 minutes.

Raise speed to high; beat until stiff peaks form.

What does 'stiff peaks' mean? That's when you lift out the whisk attachment and the egg whites on the end of it come to a point without folding over on themselves. (Those would be soft peaks.)

Reduce speed to medium-low and switch to paddle attachment. Add whipped butter, 2-3 tablespoons at a time, until fully incorporated.

QUEST REQUIREMENTS:

1 ½ lbs (680 grams) melted and cooled semi-sweet chocolate

½ cup + 1 tablespoon unsweetened cocoa powder

½ cup + 1 tablespoon boiling water

2 ¼ cup salted butter

¾ cup icing sugar

Hand or stand mixer

Piping bag

Piping tip (as listed in the individual recipe)

SKILL CHECK:

Not using all the frosting right away? The remainder can be stored in an airtight container in the fridge for up to five days, or frozen for up to a month. Bring to room temperature and beat slowly until smooth when ready to use. (Frosting may lighten in color when re-whipped, but will still be just as delicious!)

DARK CHOCOLATE FROSTING

You pass through the tattered old gates of a once bustling township and head toward the house high on the hill, home to a powerful witch, now one of the town's only residents. She lets you in her front door, and when you look in her eyes, an old woman is staring back at you, not the vibrant sorceress you once knew.

"What happened?" you ask. "You've aged 50 years since we last met!"

She tells you she made a trade with a fiery-eyed baker who came to town: her youth and magics in exchange for the best chocolate frosting recipe this world has ever known.

That recipe, adventurer, is inscribed below. And yes — it's worth it.

MAKES **5 DARK AND MYSTERIOUS CUPS**

Melt chocolate in a double boiler, or carefully on stovetop at a low temperature. Once melted, set aside to cool.

In a separate bowl, combine cocoa and boiling water, stirring until cocoa has dissolved. Set aside.

Beat butter with a mixer on medium-high speed until pale and creamy, about two minutes.

Reduce speed to low. Add icing sugar and mix until incorporated. Put mixer back up to medium-high and beat until pale and fluffy, about five minutes.

Reduce speed back to low and add cooled chocolate, mixing until combined and scraping down sides and bottom of bowl with a spatula.

Beat in cocoa mixture.

Insert recommended tip into piping bag, and follow the frosting techniques as illustrated on pages 27 - 33.

QUEST REQUIREMENTS:

1 ½ cups salted butter, softened

Half brick of cream cheese, softened

5 cups icing sugar

1 teaspoon vanilla Flavoring oil
(as listed in the individual recipe)

Gel food coloring (as listed in the
individual recipe)

Stand or hand mixer

Piping bag

Piping tip (as listed in the
individual recipe)

SKILL CHECK:

*While the classic and vegan
buttercream frostings can sit at
room temperature overnight, this
cream cheese frosting should be
refrigerated in an airtight container.
Bring cupcakes to room temperature
before nomming the next day – or
sneak out to the fridge at night and
just lick all the chilled frosting off
each and every cupcake, then blame
it on the dog. I'm not here to judge.
Do it to it, adventurer.*

CREAM CHEESE FROSTING

What's better than buttercream frosting? Buttercream frosting with a generous portion of cream cheese mixed into it. Like a time-travelling Doctor and his "much-younger-but-mentally-comparable" companion, some things in this world are just meant to be thrown together.

MAKES **5 CREAMY, CHEESY CUPS**

Beat butter and cream cheese together with a mixer on medium-high speed until pale and creamy, about two minutes.

Reduce speed to low. Add sugar, half a cup at a time, beating after each addition. Once all sugar is incorporated, increase speed to medium-high and beat until fluffy, about five minutes. (Don't skimp on the mixing! The longer you whip the frosting, the more air is incorporated and the fluffier the resulting frosting.)

Mix in vanilla and any flavoring oil as recommended by the individual recipe.

Insert recommended tip into piping bag, and follow the frosting techniques as illustrated on pages 27 - 33.

1 ½ cups granulated sugar

2 tablespoons light corn syrup

¼ cup water

6 large egg whites
(do not substitute egg whites in a carton for these)

1 teaspoon vanilla

Stand mixer

Double boiler, or a mixer bowl set over a pan of simmering water

Piping bag

Piping tip (as listed in the individual recipe)

SKILL CHECK:

Don't let the raw egg whites scare you away from this classic fluffy frosting! The temperature they reach during the double boiling as well as the inclusion of a large amount of sugar makes them safe to eat. If you have a candy thermometer, your egg white mixture should reach at least 160° F, according to the Sorcerer Supreme over at the U.S. Department of Health & Human Services.

7-MINUTE FLOOFY FROSTING

This light and fluffy meringue-style frosting is as versatile as it is "floofy." Use it to pile towering tops on chocolate-dipped hi-hat cupcakes or toast it with a kitchen torch for a 'toasted marshmallow' effect.

MAKES **8 CUPS OF FLOOF**

Whisk together sugar, corn syrup, water, and egg whites in mixer bowl placed on top of a pan of simmering water. Cook, whisking constantly, until the sugar has dissolved and the mixture is warm to the touch, about two minutes *(Figure 1)*.

Attach bowl to a mixer fitted with the whisk attachment and beat on high speed until glossy and oh-so-fluffy, with stiff-peaks, *(Figure 2)*. This will take about seven minutes. Hence the name! See what they did there? Seven minutes! Beat in vanilla until combined.

(Figure 1)

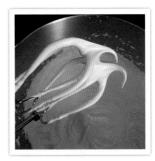

(Figure 2)

Use immediately – frosting surface will quickly harden, so insert recommended tip into piping bag and follow frosting techniques as illustrated on pages 27 - 33.

½ cup vegetable shortening
(non-hydrogenated!)

½ cup vegan margarine
(also non-hydrogenated!)

3 ½ cups powdered sugar

2 teaspoons vanilla

¼ cup soy milk
(or other non-dairy milk)

Flavoring oil (as listed in the
individual recipe)

Gel food coloring (as listed in the
individual recipe)

Stand or hand mixer

Piping bag

Piping tip (as listed in the
individual recipe)

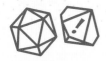

SKILL CHECK:

*If you find the buttercream is too
thick for your spreading or piping
needs, thin it out with any non-dairy
beverage or liquid creamer you
have on hand. Coconut oil will also
do the trick, but keep in mind it will
also add a noticeable (but delicious!)
coconut flavor to your frosting.*

BUTTERLESS BUTTERCREAM

*For vegan adventurers! Pair with the Vegan Chocolate
Cupcakes on page 48, or with the Vegan Vanilla Cupcakes
on page 50.*

MAKES **5 CUPS**

Add shortening and margarine to a large mixing bowl or to
bowl of a stand mixer, and mix until combined, scraping the
sides and bottom of the bowl with a spatula.

Reduce speed to low. Add sugar, half a cup at a time,
beating after each addition. Once all sugar is incorporated,
increase speed to medium-high and beat until fluffy, about
five minutes. (Don't skimp on the mixing! The longer you
whip the frosting, the more air is incorporated and the
fluffier the resulting frosting.)

If you find the frosting is too thick, add soy milk or any other
non-dairy milk beverage a tablespoon at a time, stopping
when it reaches a smooth, spreading consistency.

Mix in vanilla and any flavoring oil as listed in the
individual recipe.

Insert recommended tip into piping bag, and follow frosting
techniques as illustrated on pages 27 - 33.

¾ cup warm water

5 tablespoons meringue powder

1 teaspoon cream of tartar
(it's a thing - check the baking aisle
or with the spices)

5 cups icing sugar

Stand or hand mixer

SKILL CHECK:

*Cover unused portion with a
dampened tea towel while piping
to prevent icing from crusting over.
"But... I forgot the tea towel and it's
all crunchy on top!" you exclaim. No
worries – here's a combat trick to get
you back on top. Don't mix it back
together, or tiny crunchy bits will be
incorporated into the mix, causing
your piping tip to clog. Instead, give
it a quick spray from a clean spray
bottle filled with water and let sit
until the crusted layer softens, then
stir back together. This is also a great
way to add just enough water to get
the consistency you want.*

ROYAL ICING

MAKES **6 CUPS**

Royal icing frosts a beautiful cookie, but can be a tireless battle when it comes to consistency. Too thin, and it will run right off the cookie. Too thick, and you end up with a bumpy unattractive surface. However, there is a 'win' condition for the perfect royal icing consistency, and it's called "The 10 Second Rule".

Drag a butter knife through the surface of the royal icing and count to 10:

If the icing surface smooths out in 7-10 seconds: You win! The icing is ready to use.

If it takes longer than 10 seconds to smooth: The icing is too thick. Add a teaspoon of water and mix for a minute or so to thin out.

If it smooths over in less than 7-10 seconds: It is too runny. Mix your icing longer or slowly add more sifted icing sugar to thicken it.

Note: while this is *my* perfect icing consistency, you may find yours will vary. There are a lot of cookie peeps out there in the internets, and not one has the same technique or timing. Try it out and see what works best for you. Soon enough you'll fall into your own icing groove.

In mixer bowl, combine warm water and meringue powder. Mix with a whisk by hand until frothy and thickened, about 30 seconds.

Add cream of tartar and mix by hand for another 30 seconds.

Pour in all icing sugar at once and place the bowl on the mixer. Icing sugar does not have to be sifted.

Using the paddle attachment on the LOWEST speed, mix for a full 10 minutes. Icing will become thick and creamy.

Tint with gel food coloring and any flavoring oil as recommended by the individual recipe.

QUEST REQUIREMENTS:

2 cups salted butter, room temperature

2 cups granulated sugar

5 cups all-purpose flour

3 teaspoons baking powder

½ teaspoon salt

2 large eggs

2 teaspoons vanilla

Stand or hand mixer

Rolling pin

Cookie cutter, sharp paring knife, or X-acto knife

NO-FAIL SUGAR COOKIES

For a 'perfect every time' cookie that looks like you plucked it from a portal you placed in Martha Stewart's pantry.

MAKES **4-5 DOZEN, DEPENDING ON COOKIE SIZE**

Preheat oven to 350° F.

Beat butter and sugar together with a mixer on medium-high speed until pale and creamy, about two minutes.

In a separate large bowl, whisk together dry ingredients.

Add eggs and vanilla to creamed butter and sugar. Mix well.

With mixer on lowest speed, add flour mixture a little at a time to butter mixture. Mix until the flour is completely incorporated and the dough comes together. (Dough will be crumbly. You may need to turn out the dough onto a flat surface and finish mixing it by hand.)

Roll out dough using the rolling technique outlined on page 34, and cut out with cookie cutters or cookie template. (Template instructions are on page 35.) Bake on ungreased baking sheet at 350° F for 8-10 minutes or until just beginning to turn brown around the edges.

½ cup salted butter,
room temperature

1 tablespoon vegetable oil

1/3 cup granulated sugar

1 teaspoon vanilla

½ teaspoon salt

1 large egg

¼ cup cornstarch

½ cup unsweetened cocoa powder

1 ¼ to 2 cups all-purpose flour

Stand or hand mixer

Rolling pin

Cookie cutter, sharp paring knife,
or X-acto knife

CHOCOLATE SUGAR COOKIES

Not feeling the classic vanilla cookie? Looking to impress a certain half-demon cutie who has a sweet dragon familiar and a love of all things chocolate? Take a walk on the dark side with these rich chocolate sugar cookies.

MAKES 3-4 DOZEN, DEPENDING ON COOKIE SIZE

Preheat oven to 350° F.

Beat butter, oil, sugar, vanilla, and salt with a mixer on medium-high speed until mixture is smooth, about a minute.

Add the egg and mix until incorporated, then add cornstarch, cocoa powder, and 1 ¼ cups of the flour. Continue adding flour until the dough begins to form a ball and come away from the sides of the mixer bowl – you may not need to incorporate all the flour.

Roll out dough using the rolling technique outlined on page 34, and cut out with cookie cutters or cookie template. (Template instructions are on page 35.) Bake on ungreased baking sheet at 375° F for 10-12 minutes, or until cookie surfaces look dry and feel firm around the edges and are set in the middle.

SQUIRE

"Starter quests to begin your baking adventure."

QUEST REQUIREMENTS:

*Moist Chocolate Cupcakes recipe
(see page 44)*

*Classic Buttercream recipe
(see page 58)*

Peppermint flavoring oil

1 bag chocolate chips

1 cup dark chocolate candy melts

*Piping bag with large star tip +
an additional piping bag*

*Cupcake liners (green or
black recommended)*

Green gel food coloring

SKILL CHECK:

*Melted chocolate = sticky chocolate.
But once drizzled onto the frosting,
the candy melt will quickly begin to
set and the chocolate chips will no
longer stick. For that reason, sprinkle
the chocolate chips immediately
after each drizzle: drizzle, sprinkle,
drizzle, sprinkle, driz — you see what
I'm getting at here.*

MINT CONDITION CUPCAKES

*We all know it's a sin to take it out of the package.
But you won't be able to resist with these minty, melty,
delicious cupcakes. So go for it, adventurer – eBay resale
value be damned.*

MAKES **30-32 CUPCAKES**

Preheat oven to 350° F, and line cupcake tins with cupcake liners.

Prepare the Moist Chocolate Cupcakes recipe (see page 44). Once batter is complete, mix in one-half teaspoon of peppermint flavoring (or more to taste.)

Fill cupcake liners two-thirds of the way to the top with a disher or spoon. Bake 15-20 minutes, until a wooden toothpick inserted into the center of the cupcake comes out clean. Carefully remove cupcakes from the pan and allow to come to room temperature.

Prepare the Classic Buttercream recipe (see page 58.)

Tint buttercream with green gel food coloring by adding coloring to buttercream with a toothpick. (No double dipping!) Mix to incorporate color.

Add 15-20 drops of peppermint flavoring to buttercream with an eyedropper, and mix until combined. Add more flavoring to taste. Not minty enough for you? More flavoring drops!

When cupcakes are cool, frost a **classic rosette** on top with large star tip. (See page 27 for frosting technique.)

Add one cup of dark chocolate candy melts to a piping bag with no tip and twist closed, sealing with an elastic. Place in microwave and heat briefly until just melted, about 30 seconds to a minute.

Snip off the very tip of the piping bag, and drizzle the chocolate onto the frosting with a quick back-and-forth motion. Sprinkle on chocolate chips.

QUEST REQUIREMENTS:

Foolproof Vanilla Cupcakes recipe
(see page 42)

Brown Sugar Swiss Meringue
Buttercream (see page 60)

1 bag mini chocolate chips

24 mini chocolate chip cookies

For the Cookie Dough Filling:

4 tablespoons salted butter,
room temperature

6 tablespoons brown sugar, packed

1 cup + 2 tablespoons all-purpose flour

7 ounces sweetened condensed milk

½ teaspoon vanilla

¼ cup mini chocolate chips

Piping bag with large star tip

Cupcake liners (gold or white
recommended)

Cupcake corer (optional)

THE BREAK-CUP

All quests can be treacherous, sometimes to "the feels." Has a handsome rogue run away with the contents of your bag of holding — and your heart along with it? Then this is just the cupcake to push those feelings way, waaaay down to the bottom of your stomach.

Vanilla cake stuffed with a mouthful of sinful raw cookie dough, topped with a smooth brown sugar swiss meringue buttercream, chocolate chips, and a mini chocolate chip cookie. Uungh, YES.

MAKES **22-25 CUPCAKES IN WHICH TO DROWN SORROWS**

Preheat oven to 350° F, and line cupcake tins with cupcake liners.

Prepare the Foolproof Vanilla Cupcakes recipe (see page 42)

Fill cupcake liners two-thirds of the way to the top with a disher or spoon. Bake 18 minutes, or until a wooden toothpick inserted into the center of the cupcake comes out clean. Carefully remove from the cupcake pan and allow to come to room temperature.

Prepare the Cookie Dough Filling:

Combine butter and brown sugar in a mixing bowl and cream on medium-high speed until light and fluffy, about two minutes.

Beat in flour, sweetened condensed milk, and vanilla until incorporated and smooth. Use less or more sweetened condensed milk as necessary to help make the consistency close to cookie dough. Mix in the mini chocolate chips.

Cover with plastic wrap and refrigerate until the mixture has firmed up a bit, about an hour.

When cupcakes are cooled, use a knife or a cupcake corer to remove a small amount of cake from the center of the cupcake *(Figure 1)*. Feel free to nom immediately, or put in a ziplock bag in the freezer for future cake pops. (See page 52). Use a mini scoop or your hands to portion out prepared Cookie Dough Filling into bite-sized balls. Remainder can

---

be put on a cookie sheet until frozen, then stored in a ziplock bag in the freezer for two or three months.

Insert Cookie Dough Filling balls into holes created in cupcakes *(Figure 2)*.

(Figure 1)

(Figure 2)

Prepare Brown Sugar Swiss Meringue Buttercream recipe (see page 60).

Frost cupcakes with **flat rosette** using a large star tip (see page 28 for frosting technique), sprinkle with chocolate chips, and top with a single mini chocolate chip cookie *(Figures 3 and 4)*.

(Figure 3)

(Figure 4)

SKILL CHECK:

For the mini chocolate chip cookies, store-bought Mini Chips Ahoy cookies will work great and are just the right size. Regular sized cookies broken in half can be used as well. You can, of course, bake tiny chocolate chip cookies from scratch. However, this will require you to add +10 to the "Show-Off" stat on your character sheet.

QUEST REQUIREMENTS:

¼ cup salted butter

1 bag marshmallows, standard size
(about 40 marshmallows)

1 teaspoon vanilla

Green gel food coloring

Black gel food coloring

6 cups crisped rice cereal

2-inch ball of chocolate fondant

Creeper Crispies template

Plastic (not latex) gloves

9 x 13 inch baking pan

Waxed paper

CREEPER CRISPIES

As you journey ever forward in your baking quest, you hear a growing hissing behind you: you work up the courage to turn around, clutching your meager blade in your quivering, sweaty palm, and see a mighty Creeper towering over you!

But all is well, adventurer. He just wants you to make some crisped rice cereal treats in his image for a Creeper sleepover he's hosting. He's actually a swell guy.

MAKES **12 SQUARES, CREEPY AND CRISPY**

In a large saucepan over low heat, melt butter. Add marshmallows; stir until melted and well blended. Remove from heat.

Stir in vanilla and green dye until desired green color is reached *(Figure 1)*. Add cereal, stirring until coated. It takes a good amount of stirring to cover all the cereal completely *(Figure 2)*. Just when you think you're done, keep going a little longer!

(Figure 1)

(Figure 2)

Rub a tiny bit of butter on your hands to make them non-stick, and press mixture into a 9 x 13 inch pan lined with waxed paper. Re-apply butter to 'de-stick' hands as required. Cool pan and contents in fridge.

While squares are cooling, don your stylish plastic gloves and tint some chocolate fondant with black gel food coloring. Roll out to one-eighth of an inch thick on waxed paper, and let dry for one hour.

Print Creeper Crispies template (visit books.geeksweets.net to print templates), and trace 3 shapes onto a piece of wax paper. Cut shapes out of wax paper with scissors. Place a tiny dot of butter on cut wax paper template to stick to fondant, then cut around edge with a sharp knife. Repeat until you have 12 sets of 3. For more details on how to use fondant with templates, check out the Custom Edible Toppers tutorial on page 204.

Once cool, remove the squares from the pan by grabbing the edges of the waxed paper. Flip squares over and slowly peel off the waxed paper. (Don't rush it! Or you'll end up with little bits of waxed paper stuck to the squares, and the Creepers will be most unimpressed.)

Cut squares into twelve 3 x 3 inch squares. You'll see you're left with an additional 1 x 9 inch piece. That's for you, adventurer! You've come this far – you deserve it.

Press the fondant face pieces in place on top of each square, then flip square over and press down onto a clean, flat countertop to press them even further into place. Store in a plastic container between pieces of waxed paper until they're handed off to the Creeper and his bros.

SKILL CHECK:

Feeling lazy? What squire doesn't, every now and then? Let's microwave the marshmallows to save some time. Start by microwaving the butter at full power for 30 to 60 seconds or until melted. Add marshmallows, tossing to coat. Microwave at full power 1-1 ½ minutes, stirring after 45 seconds. Stop when smooth and completely melted. Follow remaining steps as listed.

QUEST REQUIREMENTS:

*Foolproof Vanilla Cupcakes recipe
(see page 42)*

*Classic Buttercream recipe
(see page 58)*

1 cup peanuts, chopped

½ cup creamy peanut butter

1 tablespoon vanilla

1 jar marshmallow fluff

½ cup dark chocolate candy melts

15 large marshmallows

*2 piping bags, 1 intact and
one fitted with large star tip*

*Cupcake liners
(white recommended)*

SKILL CHECK:

*Don't worry about trying to get the
majority of the chocolate to drip
off the dipped marshmallow before
plopping it on top of the cupcake.
Part of this cupcake's charm is the
chocolate dripping down over
the buttercream.*

FLUFFERNUTTER CUPCAKES

*Aside from being an excellent nickname for a cat, a
Fluffernutter is a sugar bomb of a sandwich advertised
on the side of a jar of marshmallow fluff – peanut
butter and marshmallow sandwiched between two
slices of moist white bread. Recreate this monstrosity
of a sandwich with the cupcake recipe below, then top
it off with a chocolate-dipped marshmallow for a little
added flair. Because we're fancy like that.*

MAKES **22-25 FLUFFY NUTTY CUPCAKES**

Preheat oven to 350° F; line cupcake tins with cupcake liners.

Prepare the Foolproof Vanilla Cupcakes recipe (see page 42.)

Fill cupcake liners two-thirds of the way to the top with a
large ice cream scoop or a spoon. Bake 15-20 minutes, until
a wooden toothpick inserted into the center of the cupcake
comes out clean. Carefully remove from the cupcake pan
and allow to come to room temperature.

Prepare the Classic Buttercream recipe (see page 58.)

Add peanut butter and vanilla to the buttercream and mix
until combined. Add more or less peanut butter to taste.
Do not use crunchy peanut butter, as it will be more difficult
to pipe from a piping bag.

When cupcakes are cooled, use a knife or a cupcake corer
to remove a small amount of cake from the center of the
cupcake. Feel free to nom immediately, or put in a ziplock
bag in the freezer for future cake pops. (See page 52).

Fill a piping bag with marshmallow fluff, cut off the tip,
and use to fill the holes made in the cupcakes *(Figure
1)*. Marshmallow fluff, while delicious, is an ooey-gooey
disaster – hence the piping bag. You can use a spoon and
a finger covered with a light coating of margarine to fill the
cupcakes, just have some damp paper towels standing by!

Frost cupcakes with a **classic rosette**, using a large star tip,
and set aside. (See page 28 for frosting techniques.)
Cut marshmallows in half diagonally and set aside *(Figure 2*

(Figure 1)

(Figure 2)

Add dark chocolate candy melts to a microwave-safe bowl and microwave in 30 second intervals until melted, stirring after each interval.

Melt the bottom half of one of the cut marshmallows into the chocolate and immediately press it into the top of the cupcake. While the chocolate is still wet, sprinkle with chopped peanuts *(Figures 3 and 4)*.

(Figure 3)

(Figure 4)

QUEST REQUIREMENTS:

Moist Chocolate Cupcake recipe
(see page 44)

Classic Buttercream recipe
(see page 58)

½ cup chopped walnuts

⅓ cup shredded coconut

5 tablespoons Bird's Custard Powder

½ cup dark chocolate candy melts

Piping bag with large round tip

Cupcake liners (brown or
black recommended)

NANAIMO BAR CUPCAKES

*I know what you're thinking, adventurer - what the heck
is a Nanaimo?*

*Well, if you've spoken with the bravest of warriors, those
who have ventured north to the wilds of "CA-NA-DA",
then you've likely heard tales of a layered dessert – one
with a chocolate top layer, a creamy yellow middle layer of
unknown origin, and a crunchy, nutty base.*

*"How do we make a bar into a cupcake?" you ask.
"Where does the crunch come from? What makes the
middle yellow? Seriously, where is Nanaimo?" For the
answers to your questions, let's journey onward.*

MAKES **32-34 CUPCAKES**

Preheat oven to 350° F; line cupcake tins with cupcake liners.

Prepare the Moist Chocolate Cupcake recipe (see page 44).
Once batter is complete, add in the chopped walnuts and
shredded coconut, mixing just until combined.

Fill cupcake liners two-thirds of the way to the top with
a disher or spoon. Bake 15-20 minutes, until a wooden
toothpick inserted into the center of the cupcake comes out
clean. Carefully remove from the cupcake pan and allow to
come to room temperature.

Prepare the Classic Buttercream recipe (see page 58.)

Once the buttercream is prepared, mix Bird's Custard
Powder with one or two tablespoons of hot water in a small
dish – just enough to make it a darker yellow color, and
create a texture that is thick, creamy, and can be stirred
with a spoon. Mix into buttercream. Add additional custard
powder to taste.

When cupcakes are cool, frost a **flat top** with large round
tip. (see page 28 for frosting techniques.)

Let cupcakes sit for 10 to 15 minutes, until tops develop a
thin crust, then use paper towel to flatten out any bumps.

Add dark chocolate candy melts to a microwave-safe bowl and microwave in 30 second intervals until melted, stirring after each interval. Allow to cool 5-10 minutes before beginning to dip so chocolate is not so warm that it melts the frosting.

Dip the top of the cupcake in the melted candy melts, until about half of the frosting is covered *(Figures 1 and 2)*. A quick 'wiggle' of the cupcake once upright can help level out the chocolate shell. The candy melt will set quickly once on the cupcake. If the candy melts in your bowl start to harden before you've finished topping the cupcakes, simply reheat in the microwave.

(Figure 1)

(Figure 2)

SKILL CHECK:

Bird's Custard Powder: it's one of those ingredients that you never knew existed, and that you will likely only ever use for making these cupcakes and perhaps some actual Nanaimo bars. You'll find it in the baking aisle of your local supermarket. It's there, I assure you, probably down near the bottom, calling out to shoppers as they walk by, dust-covered but hopeful, waiting to fulfil its one and only glorious, creamy purpose.

Oh, and Nanaimo is in British Columbia, BTW.

— LEVEL 1 —
SQUIRE

QUEST REQUIREMENTS:

Foolproof Vanilla Cupcakes recipe
(see page 42)

Classic Buttercream recipe
(see page 58)

¼ cup instant coffee crystals

Brown gel food coloring

Chocolate covered coffee beans

3 piping bags, 2 intact, 1 fitted with
a large star tip

Cupcake liners
(brown recommended)

#SENDCOFFEE CUPCAKES

You've been gaming for 13 hours straight and your stamina is dangerously low – it's time to invoke the magnificent power of an ancient elixir gamers have been using for years to increase their stats across the board – caffeine.

MAKES **22-25 CUPCAKES**

Preheat oven to 350° F; line cupcake tins with cupcake liners.

Prepare the Foolproof Vanilla Cupcakes recipe (see page 42) to the point when batter is complete.

In a small bowl, add a few drops of hot water to instant coffee crystals – just enough to dissolve the crystals. Add half the mixture to the batter and fold in with a spatula until a marble effect is achieved *(Figure 1)*.

(Figure 1)

Fill cupcake liners two-thirds of the way to the top with a large ice cream scoop or a spoon. Bake 15-20 minutes, until a wooden toothpick inserted into the center of the cupcake comes out clean. Carefully remove from the cupcake pan and allow to come to room temperature.

Prepare the Classic Buttercream recipe (see page 58) with two tablespoons of vanilla flavoring.

Remove about half of the buttercream from the mixing bowl and reserve for later. Add the rest of the dissolved

Geek Sweets ✓
@geeksweettweets

That moment when your party's rogue rolls a crit fail on their dexterity lockpick check and instead pokes out their own eye with the lockpick tools.
#WeAreGonnaBeHereAwhile #SendCoffee

1:30 AM · 12 Aug 17

20 RETWEETS   1,009 LIKES

coffee crystals to the remaining buttercream in the mixing bowl. Add brown gel food coloring to the reserved buttercream to create a lighter brown shade then the buttercream you added the dissolved coffee crystals to. Create a two-color piping bag with the directions from page 31
(Figure 1 and 2).

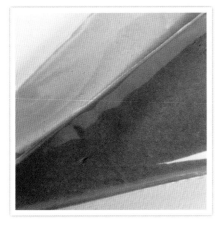

(Figure 1)

(Figure 2)

When cupcakes are cooled, frost with two-flavor buttercream in a **classic rosette** using a large star tip (see page 28 for frosting techniques.)

Top with a chocolate covered coffee bean

SKILL CHECK:

What wizardry is this? This recipe uses a magical two-flavor frosting technique that creates a visually appealing two-tone swirl. To learn this technique, handed down from the "Ancient Ones" of Baking, climb the mountain of Buttercreamia and speak to the reclusive elders perched atop its peaks.

OR, refer to the multicolor frosting technique outlined on page 31 of this book.

QUEST REQUIREMENTS:

*Foolproof Vanilla Cupcakes recipe
(see page 42)*

*Classic Buttercream recipe
(see page 58)*

Yellow and pink gel food coloring

Rainbow sprinkles

2-inch ball of white fondant

*1 piping bag, fitted with a
large star tip*

*Cupcake liners
(pink recommended)*

Plastic (not latex!) gloves

WOKKA WOKKA WOKKACAKES

No quarters necessary to hang out with this first lady of the arcade. Just don't be surprised if all you do together is run from ghosts. She has a type.

MAKES **22-25 CUPCAKES**

Preheat oven to 350° F; line cupcake tins with cupcake liners.

Prepare the Foolproof Vanilla Cupcakes recipe
(see page 42.)

Fill cupcake liners two-thirds of the way to the top with a large ice cream scoop or a spoon. Bake 15-20 minutes, until a wooden toothpick inserted into the center of the cupcake comes out clean. Carefully remove from the cupcake pan and allow to come to room temperature.

While cupcakes are cooling, prepare the Classic Buttercream recipe (see page 58) with two tablespoons of vanilla.

Tint buttercream with yellow gel food coloring by adding coloring to buttercream with a toothpick. (No double dipping!) Mix to incorporate color.

When cupcakes are cooled, frost a **classic rosette** with buttercream using a large star tip (see page 28 for frosting techniques.) Sprinkle immediately with rainbow sprinkles.

With plastic gloves on, tint fondant bright pink. Create bow shape by making a rectangle and pinching in the middle together. *(Figure 1).* Wrap a small piece of fondant around the middle, and add to top of cupcake, tilted slightly *(Figure 2).*

(Figure 1)

(Figure 2)

QUEST REQUIREMENTS:

Foolproof Vanilla Cupcakes recipe
(see page 42)
Classic Buttercream recipe
(see page 58)
2 tablespoons vanilla
1 cup marshmallow fluff
Mini marshmallows
1 packet Dream Whip topping mix
Strawberry flavoring oil
Light pink gel food coloring
2 tablespoons Disco Dust
(edible, non-toxic glitter)

1 piping bag, 1 intact, 1 fitted
with a large star tip
Cupcake liners
(pink recommended)

HELLO CUPCAKE

Moist! Fluffy! Pink! Squeeeeeee! Vanilla cake, topped with strawberry marshmallow frosting and mini marshmallows. Do you have girl parts? Then this cupcake's for you!

MAKES **22-25 SPARKLY CUPCAKES**

Preheat oven to 350° F; line cupcake tins with cupcake liners.

Prepare the Foolproof Vanilla Cupcakes recipe (see page 42)

Fill cupcake liners two-thirds of the way to the top with a disher or spoon. Bake 15-20 minutes, until a wooden toothpick inserted into the center of the cupcake comes out clean. Carefully remove from the cupcake pan and allow to come to room temperature.

Prepare the Classic Buttercream recipe (see page 58) with two tablespoons of vanilla flavoring.

Add one cup marshmallow fluff and 15 drops strawberry flavoring to the buttercream and mix until combined.

Tint buttercream with light pink gel food coloring by adding coloring to buttercream with a toothpick. (No double dipping!) Mix to incorporate color.

Put aside prepared buttercream. In a clean mixer bowl, prepare Dream Whip by following directions on package. Tint dream whip with light pink gel food coloring (just a tiny dot!) and 6-8 drops of strawberry flavoring. Fill a piping bag with the prepared strawberry-flavored Dream Whip and cut off the tip.

When cupcakes are cooled, use a knife or a cupcake corer to remove a small amount of cake from the center of the cupcake *(Figure 1)*. Feel free to nom immediately, or put in a ziplock bag in the freezer for future cake pops. (See page 52).

Fill holes in cupcakes with prepared strawberry-flavored Dream Whip *(Figure 2)*.

SQUEEEEEEEEEEEEE

(Figure 1)

(Figure 2)

Frost with buttercream in a **classic rosette** using a large star tip (see page 28 for frosting techniques.) Sprinkle immediately with a light dusting of Disco Dust by dipping a large, soft-bristled paintbrush into the container, then tapping it lightly over the frosted cupcakes (Figure 3).

Top with three mini marshmallows, (Figure 4), and bask in the fluffy marshmallowy glory of the pinkest cupcake known to humankind.

(Figure 3)

(Figure 4)

SKILL CHECK:

Disco Dust. Baking Wizards far and wide have been debating the use of this sparkling substance since the first wedding cake demanded, 'make me more sassy!' The line between 'edible' and 'just digestible' is a bit blurred, depending on who you talk to. While I wouldn't eat it by the spoonful, a light dusting can be used to give your baked goods some non-toxic sparkle.

QUEST REQUIREMENTS:

Cake Pop recipe (see page 52
for recipe and supplies)

1 package milk chocolate
candy melts

Rainbow candy-coated
chocolate chips

Assorted flavoring oils (optional)

SKILL CHECK:

*The snozberries taste
like snozberries! Interested
in recreating the mixed flavor
extravaganza from the 'wallpaper
licking' scene inside Willy Wonka's
Chocolate Factory? Mix five or six
drops of a random flavor oil into
each scoop of cake pop mixture
before rolling into a ball and have a
blast guessing which is which!*

SNOZBERRY CAKE POPS

*A simple pop to make, with a big impact – people will
think you've kidnapped an Oompa-Loompa to do your
baking bidding. If you can't find rainbow candy-coated
chocolate chips at your local bulk store, any brightly
colored candy will do – rainbow nerds or chopped mini
M&M's, for example.*

MAKES **40-50 CAKE POPS**

Follow cake pop recipe from page 52, right up until the
pops are ready to dip.

Fill a large bowl with the rainbow candy-coated chocolate
chips. Make sure it's a big bowl, otherwise candy scatters
everywhere! Take it from someone still picking candy bits
out of the toaster.

Dip pop in melted candy melts, and while the chocolate
is still wet, hold the pop over the bowl of chocolate chips.
Sprinkle handfuls over the pop, letting the excess chocolate
chips fall back into the bowl. Rotate pop as you are pouring
to cover all sides *(Figure 1)*.

Chocolate will harden fast, so only do one pop at a time. If
you find a few gaps, use a toothpick to smear on additional
melted chocolate and a pair of tweezers to fill in the gaps
with the chocolate chips *(Figure 2)*.

(Figure 1)

(Figure 2)

Pops can be stored at room temperature in a cool dry place for
up to seven days from the day the original cake was baked.

QUEST REQUIREMENTS:

*Foolproof Vanilla Cupcakes recipe
(see page 42)*

*Classic Buttercream recipe
(see page 58)*

2 tablespoons vanilla

1 cup honey roasted peanuts

½ cup creamy peanut butter

*½ cup jam, any flavor
(I like raspberry best,
but you do you, adventurer.)*

Piping bag with large star tip

*Cupcake liners (coordinate with the
color of your jam! Blue for blueberry,
pink for strawberry, etc.)*

SKILL CHECK:

*"Why not just pipe the jam
into the cupcake holes from a piping
bag? Why use a spoon like some
common cave-dwelling ghoul?" you
ask. I'll tell you why: jam is chunky.
All sorts of big fruity bits to get in
the way of your clever piping plans.
Best use a spoon, adventurer.*

PB & J CUPCAKES

Every serious adventurer knows the value of a PB & J stuffed into their Bag of Holding. After a long day of sweet-talking tavern patrons, fending off spells, and slugging goblins in the face, reaching into your bag and finding that sweet, sweet PB & J is the perfect end to your day.

But what if that sandwich… was a cupcake? Now we're talking. Short of using a transmogrification spell on your sandwich, the recipe below is just what you're looking for.

MAKES **22-25 CUPCAKES**

Preheat oven to 350° F; line cupcake tins with cupcake liners.

Prepare the Foolproof Vanilla Cupcakes recipe
(see page 42)

Fill cupcake liners two-thirds of the way to the top with a disher or spoon. Bake 15-20 minutes, until a wooden toothpick inserted into the center of the cupcake comes out clean. Carefully remove from the cupcake pan and allow to come to room temperature.

Prepare the Classic Buttercream recipe (see page 58) with two tablespoons of vanilla flavoring.

Add one quarter cup of the peanut butter to the buttercream and mix until combined. Add more peanut butter to taste if desired. Do not use crunchy peanut butter, as it will be more difficult to pipe from a piping bag.

When cupcakes are cooled, use a knife or a cupcake corer to remove a small amount of cake from the center of the cupcake. Feel free to nom immediately, or put in a ziplock bag in the freezer for future cake pops. (See page 52).

Using a spoon, fill holes in cupcakes with chosen jam flavor.

Frost cupcakes in a **classic rosette** with star tip (see page 28 for frosting techniques), and top with three honey roasted peanuts – or a whole bunch if you like a lot of crunch!

QUEST REQUIREMENTS:

Moist Chocolate Cupcake recipe
(see page 44)
Classic Buttercream recipe
(see page 58)
1 bag full-size Oreos
1 bag mini Oreos

Piping bag with medium round tip
Cupcake liners
(black recommended)

SKILL CHECK:

Make sure to press the full-size Oreo down to the bottom of the cupcake through the batter, rather than just adding it to the baking cup before adding batter. When cooled, the Oreo will still remain crunchy inside the cupcake - fancy!

COOKIES 'N CREAM CUPCAKES

Yummy and moist chocolate cake with an Oreo baked right into the base, topped with crunchy Oreo buttercream and topped with a tiny Oreo.

Did I mention there's Oreos in there?

...There's Oreos in there.

MAKES **30-32 COOKIE-STUFFED CUPCAKES**

Preheat oven to 350° F; line cupcake tins with cupcake liners.

Prepare the Moist Chocolate Cupcake recipe (see page 44)

Fill cupcake liners just under two-thirds of the way to the top with a disher or spoon, then press a single Oreo cookie all the way down to the bottom of the cupcake until it is flat against the bottom of the cupcake pan *(Figure 1 and 2)*.

(Figure 1)

(Figure 2)

Bake 15-20 minutes, until a wooden toothpick inserted into the center of the cupcake comes out clean. Carefully remove from the cupcake pan and allow to come to room temperature.

Prepare the Classic Buttercream recipe (see page 58.)

Place the remaining full-size Oreos into a large zip-top freezer bag (or any other plastic bag with the top sealed), and crush with a rolling pin. Mix into buttercream until just combined. Do not over-mix or frosting will turn grey! When cupcakes are cool, frost a **tall coil** with large round tip (see page 28 for frosting techniques), and insert a single mini Oreo cookie right on top.

QUEST REQUIREMENTS:

Foolproof Vanilla Cupcakes recipe
(see page 42)

Classic Buttercream recipe
(see page 58)

Mint flavoring

1 package dark chocolate candy melts

Gold luster dust

Gel food coloring in no-taste red,
golden yellow, blue, and green

Star Trek Starfleet Silicone Ice
Cube Tray or Cellular Peptide
Cake topper template

3 piping bags with large round tip

Large soft-bristled paintbrush

Cupcake liners (black recommended.)

SKILL CHECK:

Can't get ahold of the ice cube tray?
Geek Sweets has you covered. Print
out the Cellular Peptide Cake topper
template from books.geeksweets.
net and follow the directions on the
template for making a topper with
candy melts.

CELLULAR PEPTIDE CAKE...
WITH MINT FROSTING

Straight from your favorite shiny gold android's fever dream (no, not that gold android, the other one), it's Lieutenant Commander Worf's favorite cake!

MAKES **22-25 CUPCAKES**

Create the communicator badge toppers:

Add dark chocolate candy melts to a piping bag with no tip and twist closed, sealing with an elastic. Place in microwave and heat briefly until just melted, about 30 seconds to a minute.

Make sure silicone mold is completely clean and dry. Snip off the very tip of the piping bag and fill the silicone mold all the way to the top with melted candy melts *(Figure 1)*. (If you do not have the silicone mold, then follow the instructions on the Cellular Peptide Cake topper template to create your own. Visit books.geeksweets.net for templates.)

Carefully lift up the filled tray, and while keeping it level, tap on a flat surface to allow chocolate to settle and make any air bubbles rise to the top *(Figure 2)*.

PESKY
BUBBLE

(Figure 1)   *(Figure 2)*

Place tray in freezer for at least 20 minutes until chocolate is completely hardened.

Once hardened, carefully remove chocolate communicators by bending silicone mold to release, starting by pulling away edges. If chocolate is completely hardened, the badge

should come away easily *(Figure 3)*. You can wear chocolate handling gloves or use a piece of paper towel to help minimize the amount of fingerprints on the surface of the chocolate.

While some condensation is still on the chilled chocolate, brush on a coating of the gold luster dust using a soft paintbrush *(Figure 4)*.

(Figure 3)   *(Figure 4)*

Repeat until you have made enough chocolate communicator badges for all the cupcakes, refilling the piping bag and melting more chocolate in 30 second intervals as required. Set aside chocolate in a cool, dry place out of direct sunlight until your cupcakes are ready.

Preheat oven to 350° F; line cupcake tins with cupcake liners.

Prepare the Foolproof Vanilla Cupcakes recipe (see page 42.) Fill cupcake liners two-thirds of the way to the top with a disher or spoon. Bake 15-20 minutes, until a wooden toothpick inserted into the center of the cupcake comes out clean. Carefully remove from the cupcake pan and allow to come to room temperature.

Prepare the Classic Buttercream recipe (see page 58). Add 15-20 drops of peppermint flavoring to buttercream and mix until combined. Add more flavoring to taste. Not minty enough? More flavoring drops! Lieutenant Commander Worf likes it minty!

Divide the buttercream into 3 equal portions. You can use a kitchen scale if you have one, or just eyeball it. Dye one-third of the buttercream with the no-taste red coloring, one-third of the buttercream with golden yellow, and the last third with blue. (To get a blue that is closest to the medical branch Starfleet uniform color, add a teeny-tiny hint of green to the blue.)

Fill three piping bags outfitted with large round tips with each color of buttercream, or use one piping bag rinsed out between colors. Frost cupcakes with a **flat top** (see page 28 for frosting techniques), and top with chocolate communicator badges.

GAME NIGHT

You've completed the first level of your training! Time to lay down your sword and take a night off. Whip up the following recipes, invite over that charismatic elf archer and her friends you met at the tavern the other night, and blow the dust off your copy of Catan – it's time for a Game Night.

Visit books.geeksweets.net to print 'Game Night' invites and printables from this section!

QUEST REQUIREMENTS:

No-Fail Sugar Cookie recipe
(see page 72)

Royal Icing recipe (see page 70)

Gel food coloring in green, black,
and no-taste red

1 small tube of red decorating gel

Cthulhu Cookie template

Waxed paper

Rolling pin

Clean X-acto knife or sharp
paring knife

1 piping bag fitted with a #2 tip,
filled with green royal icing

1 piping bag fitted with a #1 tip,
filled with red royal icing

SKILL CHECK:

*For adventurers of high-level
sanity only.*

CTHULHU COOKIES

*Witness the impressive progress of your baking powers
in this next endeavor, adventurer. Harness the power
of the mighty Cthulhu – the very sound of his wing flap
is enough to drive fear into the heart of any man – and
tear him down until he is no more than just the cutesiest,
wootsiest, itty-bitty wittle Elder God there ever was!
Who's a good creature of eternity? You are! Youuu
aaaare! <Insert smoochie noises here.>*

MAKES **4-5 DOZEN ADORABLE GREAT OLD ONES**

Prepare the No-Fail Sugar Cookie recipe as directed on
page 72, to the point where dough is ready to roll out.

Roll out dough and cut into shapes, *(Figures 1 and 2),* using
the Cthulhu Cookie template and the cookie dough rolling /
cutting instructions from page 34. (Visit books.geeksweets.
net to print template.)

(Figure 1)   (Figure 2)

Bake cookies at 350° F for 8-10 minutes or until just
beginning to turn brown around the edges. Carefully
remove from baking sheet and allow to cool completely.

Prepare Royal Icing recipe from page 70 while cookies are
cooling. Remove one-third cup of frosting and dye it with
no-taste red. Store in a sealed container or a bowl covered
with a wet cloth. Set aside. To the remaining frosting,
add green gel dye with a few tiny dots of black to darken
the green shade. Fill piping bags as listed in the quest
requirements, following the directions on page 27.
Frost cookie with green royal icing, using the 'dam and

flood' cookie frosting technique from page 36, *(Figures 3 and 4)*. Complete with remaining cookies and allow to dry completely, at least one hour.

(Figure 3)

(Figure 4)

Tint remaining green icing with a bit more black, then pipe outlined Cthulhu shape, adding two feet, two wings, and three dangly tentacles *(Figures 5, 6 and 7)*. Using either the red frosting in a piping bag fitted with a #1 tip or the red decorating gel, make two dots for eyes that stare into your soul *(Figure 8)*.

(Figure 5)

(Figure 6)

(Figure 7)

(Figure 8)

Allow cookies to dry completely overnight, then store in a sealed container at room temperature between pieces of waxed paper. Cookies can also be frozen for up to one month.

QUEST REQUIREMENTS:

**For Health Potion
(Mediterranean Cosmo)**

1 ounce blood orange liqueur
1 ounce vodka
2 ounces cranberry juice
½ ounce lime juice
1 slice blood orange (optional)

For Mana Potion (Blue Lagoon)

1 ounce vodka
1 ounce blue curacao liqueur
2 ½ ounces lemonade
Blueberries (optional)

Ice
Cocktail shaker (or large mason jar
or container for mixing)
Small mason jars (one for each attendee)
Health and Mana Stickers

HEALTH / MANA POTION

You must be feeling pretty drained by now, adventurer – time to replenish those health and mana stores so you're in top fighting shape. Your party attendees will thank you for the top-up when the orcs start showing up with kegs full of mead and hearts full of fury. Orcs are hard to keep up with once they start drinking.

MAKES **1 HP REFILL AND 1 MP REFILL**

Health: Shake blood orange liqueur, vodka, cranberry juice, and lime juice with ice in a cocktail shaker. Strain into a mason jar or other decorative glass, decorated with a printed Health sticker. (Visit books.geeksweets.net to print stickers.) Garnish with a slice of blood orange if desired.

Mana: Pour vodka and curacao over ice in a mason jar or other decorative glass decorated with a printed Mana sticker. (Visit books.geeksweets.net to print stickers.) Fill with lemonade, drop in some blueberries if desired, and serve.

Store in the fridge until your adventuring party is running low on HP / MP mid-campaign and keep the party going!

For a non-alcoholic boost:

Use soda water, lemonade, and two teaspoons berry blue Jello powder for your Mana potion, and soda water, cranberry juice, and two teaspoons cherry Jello powder for the health potion. (Use more or less jello powder to taste.)

— LEVEL TWO —

KNIGHT

"Grinding your skills in the kitchen for maximum XP!"

QUEST REQUIREMENTS:

*Moist Chocolate Cupcake recipe
(see page 44)*

*7-Minute Floofy Frosting recipe
(see page 68)*

*1 bag semi-sweet chocolate chips
(minis melt faster!)*

3 tablespoons vegetable oil

2-inch ball chocolate fondant

1-inch ball vanilla fondant

Black gel food coloring

Gold sugar pearls

*Piping bag fitted with
medium round tip*

*Plastic microwavable cup or bowl,
deep enough for dipping*

Mesh strainer

*Cupcake liners
(brown recommended)*

Plastic gloves (not silicone!)

SKILL CHECK:

*Miss a spot at the base
of the frosting that didn't get
coated with chocolate? Use a
toothpick dipped in chocolate
to touch up any gaps.*

POOPCAKES

Not all adventuring is fun and games, you know. It's not all princesses in high towers with abnormally long hair, and treasure rooms overflowing with more crowns and chalices then one could ever need in a lifetime. Some of it's hard and dirty – throwing you face-first into a pit of danger, knee deep in… well. You know.

MAKES **30-32 POOPCAKES**

Create fondant flies:

Don your fancy plastic gloves and add black gel dye to chocolate fondant with a toothpick. Mix until combined, adding more black dye as required.

Create a small black bean shape with fondant *(Figure 1)*, and press two gold sugar pearls into fondant at one end for eyes *(Figure 2).*

(Figure 1)   (Figure 2)

Roll two small balls of white fondant, each one about one-quarter the size of the body, and press into a mesh strainer to make a wing pattern and flatten out the ball *(Figures 3 and 4).*

FEATURED DURING

CAKE WRECKS

THE "WINTER UNDERLINED" TOUR

(Figure 3)

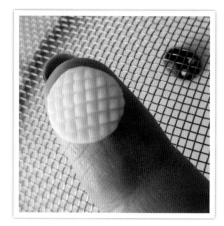
(Figure 4)

Attach wings to the body with a tiny dot of water and a toothpick, and allow to dry completely *(Figures 5 and 6)*.

(Figure 5)

(Figure 6)

Preheat oven to 350° F; line cupcake tins with cupcake liners.

Prepare the Moist Chocolate Cupcake recipe (see page 44).

Fill cupcake liners two-thirds of the way to the top with a disher or spoon. Bake 15-20 minutes, until a wooden toothpick inserted into the center of the cupcake comes out clean. Carefully remove from the cupcake pan and allow to come to room temperature.

While cupcakes are cooling, prepare the 7-Minute Floofy Frosting recipe (see page 66,) and fill a piping bag fitted with a medium round tip.

Add chocolate chips and vegetable oil to a plastic microwavable cup or bowl deep enough for dipping, then microwave in 30 second intervals until melted, stirring after each interval *(Figure 7)*.

When cupcakes are completely cool, frost with a big heaping mound of frosting about the same height as the cupcake, or even taller if you can *(Figure 8)*. Don't frost it any taller than your cup of melted chocolate is deep, or you won't be able to completely cover it with chocolate. (Follow the **tall coil** technique from page 30.)

(Figure 7)

(Figure 8)

Flip cupcake upside down (don't worry, frosting won't fall off – 7 Minute Floofy Frosting defies gravity), and submerge frosting in melted chocolate right up to where it hits the cupcake. Lift out of chocolate and set on a table right-side-up *(Figure 8 and 9)*.

(Figure 9)

(Figure 10)

Before the chocolate cools completely, press fondant fly into chocolate at the very top of the cupcake.

QUEST REQUIREMENTS:

Foolproof Vanilla Cupcakes recipe
(see page 42)

Classic Buttercream recipe
(see page 58)

1 tablespoon clear butter flavoring
(optional)

1 bag mini marshmallows

Powdered yellow food coloring

Movie Night Cupcake
Liners template

Cupcake liners
(any color will do as they will be
covered; I like to use white.)

Piping bag with large
round tip

Scissors

A color printer and 13 pieces
of cardstock

Stand or hand mixer

Large ice cream scoop or disher
(optional)

MOVIE NIGHT CUPCAKES

It may look like an imp-sized tub of popcorn, but it's actually a cupcake, covered in frosting and marshmallows, wearing a printable sleeve. Good thing, too – popcorn gives imps the toots.

MAKES **22-25 TASTY TUBS**

Preheat oven to 350° F; line cupcake tins with cupcake liners.

Prepare the Foolproof Vanilla Cupcakes recipe
(see page 42.)

Fill cupcake liners two-thirds of the way to the top with a large ice cream scoop or a spoon. Bake 15-20 minutes, until a wooden toothpick inserted into the center of the cupcake comes out clean. Remove from the cupcake pan and allow to come to room temperature.

While cupcakes are cooling, prepare the Classic Buttercream recipe (see page 58), with one tablespoon of clear butter flavoring. The buttercream will already taste 'buttery' as referenced in the name, but the clear butter flavoring will add in a bit of that 'fake movie theater butter' taste.

Prepare the 'popcorn':

Take a single mini marshmallow, and with a pair of scissors, cut halfway down the marshmallow from the top.

Rotate the marshmallow and cut halfway down the marshmallow again, creating an X-shaped cut in the top
(Figures 1 and 2).

(Figure 1) (Figure 2)

MOVIE NIGHT
C U P C A K E S

Now flip your marshmallow, and on a piece of waxed paper or other clean surface, smoosh that little fellah down with your finger. Smoosh down hard and wiggle it in little circles for about three seconds *(Figure 3)*.

When flipped back over, your marshmallow will have the look of a piece of popcorn! You can mix it up a bit, cutting some marshmallows only once or into three sections instead of two, in order to make the popcorn look varied *(Figure 4)*.

(Figure 3)

(Figure 4)

Continue until you have done so with the whole bag of mini marshmallows (or until you have about a third of a cup of marshmallows per cupcake baked.)

Now that you've got all your marshmallows smooshed and your cupcakes baked, it's time to print out the cupcake wrappers. Visit books.geeksweets.net to print wrappers.

Print as many copies of the template as you need onto some cardstock paper, then cut them out. It's best to use a glossy paper, because the frosted cupcakes will touch the liner, and a non-glossy paper may develop grease stains from the buttercream. Take one of your cupcakes and wrap the cupcake wrapper around it to see how big it should be. Stick the edge of the wrapper to itself using two-sided or regular clear tape. Use this one as a template for sizing the rest.

Pop your cupcakes into the wrappers. They should be nice and tight at the top so they don't shift around in the wrapper when picked up. You may need to press the cupcake down into the wrapper a bit with the palm of your hand. (The bottom of your cupcake and the bottom of the liner don't need to line up, so don't squish it down too far.)

With your prepared buttercream, frost a **flat top** using a large round tip (see page 28 for frosting techniques). They will not need a large amount of frosting – just enough to hold the marshmallows in place on top.

Press your prepared marshmallows into the frosting. They should be close enough together so you barely see the frosting underneath. After completely covering the top in marshmallows, smoosh them down with your palm so they make a nice, even mound on top of the cupcake.

Lastly, add the 'butter' by brushing on some yellow dye with a large, soft paintbrush - heavy in some areas, none in others, just like real movie theatre popcorn.

SKILL CHECK:

Powdered food coloring can be a little more difficult to get ahold of if you're not near a bakery supply store. It can be ordered online, but if you need a quick fix, you can thin out a little yellow gel food coloring with water and 'dry brush' yellow areas onto the marshmallows for a similar effect. In a pinch, yellow lemonade Kool-Aid could also be used, but it is not quite as vibrant and will taste of, well, yellow lemonade Kool-Aid.

QUEST REQUIREMENTS:

No-Fail Sugar Cookie recipe (see page 72) or Chocolate Sugar Cookie recipe (see page 74)

Royal Icing recipe (see page 70)

Red and black gel food coloring

Web-Slinger Cookie Pop template

Lollipop sticks

1 piping bag filled with black royal icing, fitted with #1 tip

1 piping bag filled with white royal icing, fitted with #2 tip

1 piping bag filled with red royal icing, fitted with #2 tip

Waxed paper

WEB-SLINGER COOKIE POPS

"Spider-pop, Spider-pop, does whatever a Spider-pop does. Can it swing, from a web? No, it can't, it's a pop."

MAKES **4-5 DOZEN POPS, DEPENDING ON SIZE**

Prepare the No-Fail Sugar Cookie recipe (or Chocolate Sugar Cookie recipe) to the point where dough is ready to roll out.

Roll out dough using instructions on page 34 and cut into 3-inch rounds. You can use a round cookie cutter if you have it, or use the provided circle on the cookie pop template. (Visit books.geeksweets.net for template.)

Place circles on cookie sheet with enough room to set a lollipop stick next to them. You may only be able to fit four cookies on each cookie sheet. With the lollipop stick flat against the cookie sheet, slide it up into the cookie dough. You can press your hand down on the top of the cookie while pushing, to avoid breaking through the dough. Depending on how thick you rolled your cookie dough, you may see a ridge where the stick is sitting, which is A-OK. You won't notice the ridge when the cookie is frosted.

Bake at 350° F for 8-10 minutes or until just beginning to turn brown around the edges.

While cookies are cooling, create spidey eyes out of royal icing, by making a Royal Icing Transfer! Fancy! Here's how:

First, download and print a few copies of the spidey eyes template in black and white. (Visit books.geeksweets.net for template.) Lay out your printed templates with a piece of waxed paper overtop, waxy-side up. (There's a side that's less waxy – who knew?) Use tape to hold both in place. I like doing it on a plastic tray I "forever-borrowed" from a Harvey's so I can easily rotate it as I work.

Next, outline the eyes in black with your itty bitty #1 tip. Once dry, fill in the white middles. Make a few more than you will need in case they break when lifting them off the waxed paper.

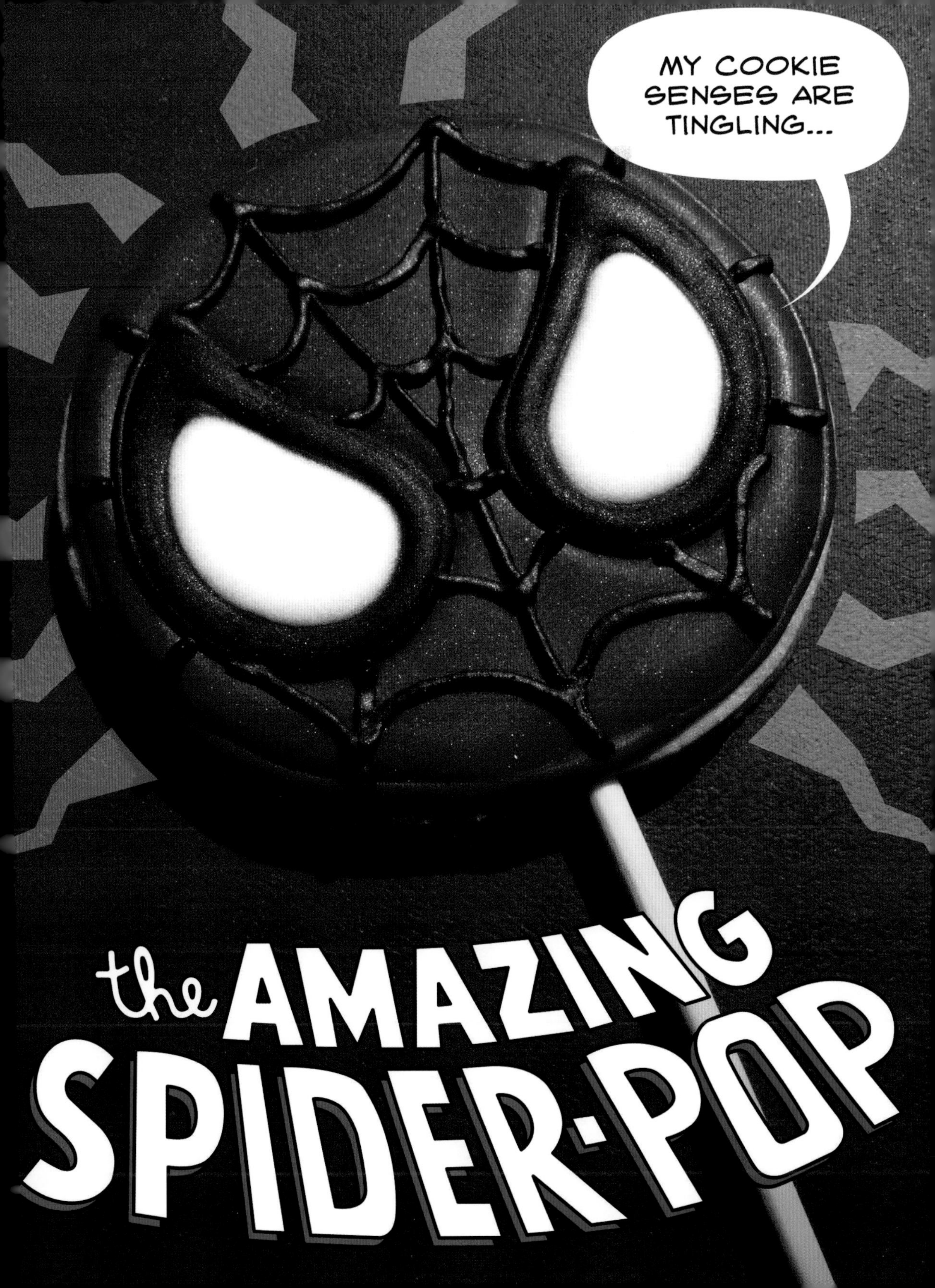
MY COOKIE SENSES ARE TINGLING...
the AMAZING SPIDER-POP

Allow to dry completely before peeling away from waxed paper *(Figures 1 and 2)*.

(Figure 1)

(Figure 2)

Frost one cookie at a time with red royal icing, using the 'dam and flood' cookie frosting technique from page 36. While the icing is still wet, take a set of dried spidey eyes and place them onto your cookie. I like to hold the eye over the top of the cookie, get it into position, then just let go and let it drop into place *(Figures 3 and 4)*.

(Figure 3)

(Figure 4)

Once they're dry, you're ready to pipe the webbing. Use your #1 black tip again – nothing bigger, or the lines will look too thick. I start with a 'Y' shape in the middle of his face and go from there *(Figures 5 and 6)*.

(Figure 5)

(Figure 6)

Allow cookies to dry overnight, then store in a sealed container at room temperature between pieces of waxed paper.

SKILL CHECK:

Be warned, adventurer – you'll want to wait until the cookies are completely cooled before attempting to lift them off the cookie sheet using a cookie lifter. And don't try to lift them up by the stick! It's a foolish venture that will only end in tears. If you do end up losing one, cover the end of the lollipop stick in royal icing, set it back in the hole left in the cookie, then allow to dry completely. No one need ever know of your cookie pop breaking treachery.

QUEST REQUIREMENTS:

Moist Chocolate Cupcake recipe
(see page 44)

Dark Chocolate Frosting recipe
(see page 62)

1 teaspoon cinnamon

½ teaspoon cayenne pepper, or
more to taste

1 cup white chocolate candy melts

Gold luster dust

White or gold nonpareils

Mayan alphabet template

Piping bag

Cupcake liners (orange or gold
recommended)

Wax paper

Clean paintbrush

MAYAN CHOCOLATE CUPCAKES

Carry one of these around if you ever need it to swap it in for a golden idol in your classic Mayan temple booby-trap situation. And if the wall of spears gets you first, at least the sweet heat of this rich, flavorful cupcake will be the last flavor on your tongue.

MAKES **30-32 SWEET AND SPICY CUPCAKES**

Preheat oven to 350° F; line cupcake tins with cupcake liners.

Create the cupcake toppers:

Visit books.geeksweets.net and print a copy of the Mayan Alphabet Template. Tape to a table, then tape a piece of wax paper overtop of the template.

Add one cup of white chocolate candy melts to a piping bag with no tip and twist closed, sealing with an elastic. Place in microwave and heat briefly until just melted, about 30 seconds to a minute.

Snip off the very tip of the piping bag and slowly trace the letters into the wax paper, using the printed template as a guide. Add nonpareils in a few areas before chocolate sets *(Figure 1).* Work one symbol at a time, as the candy melts will start to set quickly at room temperature.

Once hardened, brush the letters with the gold luster dust and a small paintbrush *(Figure 2).*

(Figure 1)

(Figure 2)

Prepare the Moist Chocolate Cupcake recipe (see page 44). Once batter is complete, add in the cinnamon and cayenne

pepper. Make sure to mix well! No one wants to hit a pocket of pure cayenne pepper in their cupcake!

Taste the batter to determine the level of heat. There should be a noticeable but faint 'burn' in your throat. Once baked, the spiciness level will actually decrease, so be brave, squire!

Fill cupcake liners two-thirds of the way to the top with a disher or spoon. Bake 15-20 minutes, until a wooden toothpick inserted into the center of the cupcake comes out clean. Carefully remove from the cupcake pan and allow to come to room temperature.

While cupcakes are baking, prepare the Rich Dark Chocolate Frosting recipe (see page 62.)

When cupcakes are cool, frost a **flat top** with large round tip (see page 28 for frosting techniques) and top with chocolate letter.

SKILL CHECK:

Feeling fearless, adventurer? Here's a pro tip that will up your luster dust game: Set a pot of boiling water on the stove and bring to a low boil. Once set, take your sheet of dry candy melt letters and flip it upside down – don't worry, your letters won't fall off! Very quickly, wave it over the steam from the boiling water. The condensation it leaves on the letters will help the luster dust stick and appear even more opaque. Fancy!

QUEST REQUIREMENTS:

Foolproof Vanilla Cupcakes recipe
(see page 42)

Classic Buttercream recipe
(see page 58)

Zest of 2 oranges

Rose flavoring, or ½ cup rosewater

Pistachio flavoring

½ cup coarsely chopped pistachios

Honey

Pink gel food coloring

Blue and yellow gel food coloring
(I like to use this instead of the
pre-mixed green, in order to get
something closer to a
pistachio color.)

Piping bag with large round tip

Cupcake liners
(pink recommended)

EAST MEETS ZEST CUPCAKES

You've traversed the desert, scorching sands biting at your heels for hours, and have reached your destination. You pull back the flap on the tent you're sure has to be a mirage, a mystic haze flowing out to reveal the master sorceress inside, levitating a few inches above the ground. On her hand is an oven mitt. You tell her you're ready to feast on the ancient knowledge she is willing to impart.

"Yes," she says. "I can see you are starving for the truth. But first – dessert."

MAKES **22-25 CUPCAKES**

Preheat oven to 350° F; line cupcake tins with cupcake liners.

Prepare the Foolproof Vanilla Cupcakes recipe (see page 42), adding orange zest and 15-20 drops of rose flavoring. Start low with the rose flavoring and taste-test as you add more, as too much can be overwhelming. However, keep in mind that the flavor will diminish slightly when baked.

Tint batter with pink gel food coloring by adding coloring to batter with a toothpick. (No double dipping!) Mix to incorporate color. A little goes a long way! A very light pink is what we're working towards.

Fill cupcake liners two-thirds of the way to the top with a disher or spoon. Bake 15-20 minutes, until a wooden toothpick inserted into the center of the cupcake comes out clean. Carefully remove from the cupcake pan and allow to come to room temperature.

While cupcakes are cooling, prepare the Classic Buttercream recipe (see page 58) and add 15-20 drops of pistachio flavoring, mixing until combined. Add more flavoring to taste. Not pistachio-y enough for you? More flavoring drops!

Tint frosting with blue and yellow gel food coloring by adding coloring to frosting with a toothpick. Alternate between green and yellow, mixing to combine between each addition, until you reach a green close to what one might call 'pistachio'.

Frost a **flat top** on the cupcakes, using a piping bag fitted with a large round tip (see page 28 for frosting techniques), and top with chopped pistachios.

Drizzle a bit of honey onto the pistachios – not too much or it will pour off the cupcake. Not that that's really a bad thing, you'll just have sticky honey fingers when eating them. There are worse things to suffer in your quest for baking wizardry, adventurer.

SKILL CHECK:

If you can't find rose flavoring, take a peek at your local Middle Eastern market. You can also use rose water: Put one-half cup of rose water on the stove and bring to a boil. Continue to simmer until liquid becomes a thicker syrup, then add cooled syrup to batter to taste.

LEVEL 2
KNIGHT

QUEST REQUIREMENTS:

Foolproof Vanilla Cupcakes recipe (see page 42)

Classic Buttercream recipe (see page 58)

Disco Dust or non-toxic glitter

Silver luster dust

Rainbow chocolate chips (rainbow sprinkles can be substituted for rainbow chips)

4-inch ball of vanilla fondant

Gel food coloring (pink, orange, yellow, and green)

Flavoring oils (optional – I used strawberry, orange, lemon, and green apple)

4 piping bags, outfitted with large star tips (or the same one, cleaned between uses)

Cupcake liners (pink, orange, yellow, and green)

Stand or hand mixer

Toothpicks

Soft paintbrush

Large ice cream scoop or disher (optional)

UNICORN CUPCAKES

Every adventurer needs a steed, and now that you've reached the level of Knight, that steed should be the envy of all your peers – a rainbow colored unicorn! It's the fantasy world's equivalent of a Lamborghini, but with more glitter and filled with rainbow chocolate chips.

MAKES **22-25 MAJESTIC BEASTS**

Create the unicorn ears:

Split the 4-inch fondant ball in half and set aside half of the undyed fondant to make the unicorn horns.

Take the other half of the fondant ball and split into four equal parts. Wearing plastic (not silicone!) gloves to protect your fingers from the dye, tint each of the four portions using the instructions found on page 33, one portion pink, one orange, one yellow, and one green.

Shape six sets of ears in each color, making a 3D triangle shape that is concave on one side. Using the back end of a paintbrush will help to create the concave shape *(Figure 1)*.

Remove a small bit of white from the undyed fondant ball and press into the concave depression to make the middle of the ears *(Figure 2)*.

(Figure 1)

(Figure 2)

Create the unicorn horns:

Divide the remaining fondant into 24 equally sized balls. With each ball, create a long, tall cone around a toothpick, with some of the toothpick still sticking out of the bottom *(Figure 3)*.

Using a regular kitchen knife, the less sharp the better, roll the edge of the knife along the cone to create a groove in the horn, starting at the bottom and going all the way to the top *(Figure 4)*.

(Figure 3)

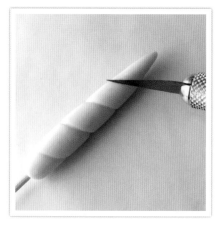

(Figure 4)

Using a soft paintbrush, dust the horns with silver luster dust *(Figure 5)*. Follow instructions for using luster dust on page 39.

(Figure 5)

Set ears and horns aside and follow the remaining instructions below.

Preheat oven to 350° F; line cupcake tins with cupcake liners, six of each color. Prepare the Foolproof Vanilla Cupcakes recipe (see page 42). When batter is complete, stir in rainbow chocolate chips.

Fill cupcake liners two-thirds of the way to the top with a disher or spoon. Bake 15-20 minutes, until a wooden toothpick inserted into the center of the cupcake comes out clean. Carefully remove from the cupcake pan and allow to come to room temperature.

While cupcakes are cooling, prepare the Classic Buttercream recipe (see page 58) with two tablespoons of vanilla flavoring, and separate into four equal parts. You can eyeball this, or use a kitchen scale to get more exact portions.

Tint each buttercream portion with gel food coloring (one pink, one orange, one yellow, and one green) by adding coloring to buttercream with a toothpick. (No double dipping!) Mix to incorporate color.

If desired, flavoring can be added to the buttercream and mixed until combined. I used strawberry in the pink frosting, orange oil in the orange frosting, lemon in the yellow frosting and green apple in the green frosting. Use 8-10 drops per portion, adding more flavoring to taste.

Frost cupcakes in a **classic rosette**, using a large star tip, six cupcakes in each color of frosting, (see page 28 for frosting techniques.) Sprinkle immediately with a light dusting of Disco Dust by dipping a large, soft-bristled paintbrush into the container, then tapping it lightly over top of the frosted cupcakes.

Top with ears in coordinating colors. Add the unicorn horn between the ears in the middle, toothpick-side down, slightly more toward the front of the cupcake.

SKILL CHECK:

When adding the rainbow chips to the batter, stir as quickly and as little as possible, as the dye on the outside of the chips will start to bleed into the batter – too much stirring and the color will blend together to an unappealing grey, as opposed to the bright rainbow bursts fitting of a fancy-pants unicorn.

QUEST REQUIREMENTS:

*Foolproof Vanilla Cupcakes recipe
(see page 42)*

*Classic Buttercream recipe
(see page 58)*

Piping bag fitted with grass tip

*Cupcake liners
(camo print, black or green)*

Mesh strainer or sifter

Plastic dollar-store army men

SKILL CHECK:

*Once you have begun the frosting
process, try not to let the tip sit open
to the air for very long, as it can
clog. If it does begin to clog, use a
toothpick to unclog. Try placing your
piping bag into a drinking glass, tip
down, with a moist paper towel at
the bottom to help keep it clog-free!*

GOT YOUR 6 CUPCAKES

*Sure, you're handy with a sword by now, adventurer, but you
never know when some weapons and combat skills might
come in handy in the Fire Swamp (those rodents aren't
kidding around.) Gather the troops for a night of Call of
Duty or Battlefront with cupcakes to match, and hone those
FPS reflexes.*

MAKES **22-25 TROOPS**

Preheat oven to 350° F; line cupcake tins with cupcake liners.

Prepare the Foolproof Vanilla Cupcakes recipe
(see page 42).

Fill cupcake liners two-thirds of the way to the top with
a disher or spoon. Bake 15-20 minutes, until a wooden
toothpick inserted into the center of the cupcake comes out
clean. Carefully remove from the cupcake pan and allow to
come to room temperature.

While cupcakes are cooling, prepare the Classic Buttercream
recipe (see page 58), sifting icing sugar before adding to
the mixer bowl. This will help avoid any solid bits that could
potentially clog your frosting tip – the grass tip is particularly
prone to clogs. Use one full quarter cup of milk to make
frosting thinner, which will also allow it to pipe easier
through the tiny holes in the grass tip. Add two tablespoons
of vanilla flavoring and mix until combined.

Tint buttercream with green gel food coloring by adding
coloring to buttercream with a toothpick. (No double
dipping!) Mix to incorporate color.

Frost cupcakes with grass tip (see page 31 for **grass
frosting technique**), and top each with a plastic army man.

QUEST REQUIREMENTS:

Cake Pops recipe using red velvet
or vanilla cake mix
(see page 52 for recipe
and supplies)

1 bag green candy melts

1 handful white candy melts

1/3 cup red candy melts

2-inch ball white fondant

Black edible ink pen

ZOMBIE CAKE POPS

You've been fighting off the undead for hours and are now trapped inside a decrepit old house with nowhere left to run. Morale is low among your party, and tummies are moaning even louder than the horde just outside the walls.

You have an idea and run to the kitchen, tearing through the pantry. "Cake mix? Check. Tub of frosting? Check…" Time to whip up a batch of zombie cake pops – turns out nothing scares off zombies quite like the sight of seeing their fellow zombie's heads impaled on sticks. And bonus: red velvet is hella delicious.

MAKES **40-50 UNDEAD HEADS ON STICKS**

Prepare cake pop mixture as detailed on page 52, and shape into misshapen balls to resemble bumpy, lumpy zombie heads *(Figure 1)*.

Roll small balls of fondant in various sizes, enough for two for each pop, and flatten with fingertip *(Figure 2)*.

(Figure 1)

(Figure 2)

Melt candy melts following melting directions in cake pop recipe, mixing green and white melts together to make a light 'zombie green' color. Dip pops as usual following directions on page 55, pressing eyes into pops while the candy is still wet *(Figure 3)*.

Using a toothpick dipped in the remaining green candy melts, add dripping blobs and smears of extra melt to the faces so it looks like your zombies have been through a rough zombie time *(Figure 4)*.

(Figure 3)

(Figure 4)

Draw on eyes and mouths with edible ink pen *(Figure 5)*. The more random the eye placement the better. You can also add different expressions with both 'angry' and 'sad' eyebrows.

Melt red candy melts and, using a toothpick, dab and drip on bits of red to resemble head wounds or bloody eyes and mouths *(Figure 6)*.

(Figure 5)

(Figure 6)

Store cake pops for up to one week in a cool, dry place.

QUEST REQUIREMENTS:

*Foolproof Vanilla Cupcakes recipe
(see page 42)*

*Classic Buttercream recipe
(see page 58)*

4 Earl Grey tea bags

1 cup 2% milk

2mm silver dragées

3-inch ball, vanilla fondant

Gold luster dust

Steampunk Cupcakes template

Lollipop stick or chopstick

Eyedropper

*1 piping bag, fitted with a
large round tip*

*Cupcake liners ('Wilton Wave'
baking cups as pictured, or any
black baking cup)*

STEAMPUNK LONDON FOG CUPCAKES

Armor feeling a little drab lately? Time to upgrade to the new (old?) style that everyone is rocking in town. Leather, lace, parasols, and gears galore – that's the ticket, old chap! Now to get working on that moustache.

MAKES **22-25 CUPCAKES**

Add milk and tea bags to a pot over medium heat. Allow to simmer until about a third of the milk has boiled off and the tea has steeped into the milk, making it a rich tan color *(Figure 1)*. Remove tea bags and set aside for later use.

Create fondant gears:

Roll fondant out about one-eighth of an inch thick, then print and use Steampunk Cupcakes template, according to instructions on page 35. (Visit books.geeksweets.net to print template.)

Paint cogs on one side with gold luster dust according to instructions on page 39. Allow to dry *(Figure 2)*.

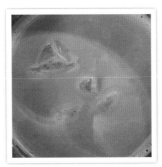

(Figure 1)   (Figure 2)

Preheat oven to 350° F; line cupcake tins with cupcake liners.

Prepare the Foolproof Vanilla Cupcakes recipe (see page 42).

Fill cupcake liners two-thirds of the way to the top with a disher or spoon. Bake 15-20 minutes, until a wooden toothpick inserted into the center of the cupcake comes out

clean. Carefully remove from the cupcake pan and allow to come to room temperature.

While cupcakes are cooling, prepare the Classic Buttercream recipe (see page 58), with two teaspoons of vanilla flavoring and five tablespoons of Earl Grey tea infused milk. A skin may have formed on the surface of the milk – remove before adding milk to frosting. Taste frosting and add more milk to taste as needed, leaving at least a half cup for the next step.

Take lollipop stick or chopstick and make four holes in the top of the cupcakes *(Figure 3)*. Fill eyedropper with a tablespoon of Earl Grey tea infused milk and squeeze into two of the four holes, rotating cupcake as you squeeze the eyedropper so that all the milk doesn't just pool in the bottom of the cupcake *(Figure 4)*. Refill eyedropper and repeat with remaining two holes.

(Figure 3)

(Figure 4)

Frost a **flat top** with buttercream using a large round tip (see page 28 for frosting techniques.) Sprinkle immediately with silver dragées. Do not allow frosting to sit for very long before sprinkling, or it will develop a crust and the dragées will just roll off the surface!

Add fondant gear to top of cupcake, gold side up.

SKILL CHECK:

If you place the cogs flat on top of the cupcake, you will not have to wait as long for the fondant to dry as with other toppers that require hardening in order to not "flop over" when coming into contact with the moisture of the buttercream.

QUEST REQUIREMENTS:

4 cups flour
2 tablespoons baking powder
1 teaspoon baking soda
1 cup granulated sugar
1 teaspoon salt
1 cup cold salted butter,
cut into small cubes
¼ cup salted butter, melted
2 cups buttermilk
Coarse sugar
20 large strawberries, washed,
with the tops cut off
½ cup strawberry jam

For the Whipped Cream Frosting:
1 cup cream cheese (½ brick),
at room temperature
¾ cup icing sugar
2 cups heavy / whipping
cream (36%)

**For the Chocolate-
DippedStrawberries:**
20 large strawberries
1 cup chocolate candy melts
½ cup pink candy melts

1 piping bag fitted with large star tip
1 intact piping bag
Cupcake liners
(pink or white recommended)
Pastry brush (optional)
Cupcake corer (optional)
Plastic microwavable cup
or bowl, deep enough for
dipping strawberries
Toothpicks or BBQ skewers (optional)
Piece of styrofoam to hold
strawberries as they dry (optional)

STRAWBERRY SHORTCAKES

Sweet, dainty, moist cakes with a stable whipped frosting and delicious strawberries. Fairies LOVE 'em. Need to catch a fairy for divining treasure and general GPS purposes? Leave a dozen of these in your backyard under a big net and wait for the giggling, glowing winged masses to descend like adorable vultures.

MAKES **18-20 MINI SHORTCAKES**

Preheat oven to 400° F; line cupcake tins with cupcake liners.

In a large bowl, combine dry ingredients.

Cut in one cup of the butter with two knives or with a pastry blender until they are combined and mixture resembles coarse oatmeal.

Add the buttermilk and mix until just moistened.

Fill cupcake liners two-thirds of the way to the top with a disher or spoon. Using the melted butter and a pastry brush (or even just your fingers), pat the top of the cupcakes with butter, then sprinkle on coarse sugar. (Regular sugar will also work, the final product will just have less of a 'crunch'.)

Bake 20 minutes, until a wooden toothpick inserted into the center of the cupcake comes out clean. Carefully remove from the cupcake pan and allow to come to room temperature.

Make the chocolate-dipped strawberries:

Add chocolate candy melts to a plastic microwave-safe bowl or cup and microwave in 30 second intervals until just melted, stirring after each interval. It should be warm, but not burning hot.

Grab strawberry by the green end, and dip into melted chocolate, dipping about three-quarters of the strawberry

Using toothpicks or long BBQ skewers, poke strawberry close to its green stem, and sit upside down in styrofoam to dry *(Figure 1)*. (You can also sit the strawberry on some wax paper, which will give it a flat bottom with some pooled chocolate around it instead, *(Figure 2),* but they'll still look fancy perched on top of the cupcake!)

(Figure 1)

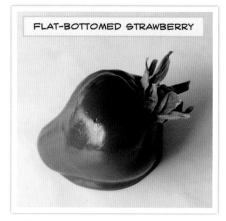

(Figure 2)

Add one-half cup pink candy melts to a piping bag with no tip and twist closed, sealing with an elastic. Place in microwave and heat briefly until just melted, about 30 seconds to a minute.

(Figure 3)

Snip off the very tippy-top of the piping bag – the tinier the opening the better! With the strawberry sitting on waxed paper, or else held by the skewer or toothpick over the waxed paper, drizzle the pink candy melt onto the strawberries with a quick back-and-forth motion (Figure 3).

When cupcakes are cooled, use a knife or a cupcake corer to remove a small amount of cake from the center of the cupcake. Feel free to nom immediately, or put in a ziplock bag in the freezer for future cake pops. (See page 52).

Add a teaspoon of strawberry jam into the hole in the cupcake, then fill the rest of the hole with one of the non-chocolate-dipped strawberries, pointy-side down. The sugar in the jam will help make the strawberry become juicy inside the cupcake, seeping into the surrounding shortcake for maximum tastiness!

Make the whipped cream topping:

With a hand or stand mixer, beat the cream cheese and icing sugar together until smooth.

Add one cup of the heavy cream, and beat until soft peaks form.

Add the remaining cup of cream, and beat until stiff peaks form. (Stiff peaks are when you lift out the whisk attachment and the cream on the end of it comes to a point without folding over on itself.)
Transfer the mixture to the prepared piping bag with a large star tip, and frost cooled / filled cupcakes with a **classic** or **princess rosette**, (see page 28 for frosting techniques).

Top each with a chocolate-dipped strawberry. If cupcakes will not be eaten that day, they should be stored overnight in the fridge in a sealed container.

SKILL CHECK:

Buttermilk – I've poured a lot of it down the sink in my time as a baking wizard. Even with constant baking going on, few recipes call for it and I can only purchase it in a large format, so it sits in the fridge, dreaming of one day being pancakes or tasty fried chicken. But the day often comes that I'm instead left to deal with its perished, stinky remains.

If you only need a small amount of buttermilk for one recipe, try this instead: Take one tablespoon of freshly squeezed lemon juice OR one tablespoon of white vinegar and add it to one cup of milk, stirring to combine. Let it sit for five minutes and BOOM – it's curdled into buttermilk! Thanks, science! Use in place of buttermilk as recipe dictates.

QUEST REQUIREMENTS:

For the Cream Cheese Mixture:

2 cups (1 8-ounce brick) cream
cheese, room temperature
1 egg, lightly beaten
1/3 cup granulated sugar
One package of mini chocolate chips

For the Black Bottoms:

1 cup granulated sugar
1 ½ cups all-purpose flour
¼ cup cocoa
1 teaspoon salt
1 cup water
½ cup vegetable oil
1 tablespoon vinegar
1 teaspoon vanilla
Classic Buttercream recipe
(see page 58)
1 tablespoon vanilla
Gel food coloring
(purple, teal and blue)
White sprinkles (nonpareils)
3-inch ball white fondant

Black edible ink pen

Gallifreyan Symbol template
Waxed paper
Small paring knife or X-acto knife

4 piping bags, 3 intact,
1 fitted with a large star tip
Cupcake liners (black recommended)

GALLIFREYAN GALAXY BLACK BOTTOM CUPCAKES

*Some say it's a dead language - but we know better.
Brush up on your skills and Gallifreyan penmanship in
order to impress everyone's favorite madman with a box.*

MAKES **18-20 CUPCAKES**

Create fondant Gallifreyan symbol toppers:

Make toppers ahead of time, or even a day before as they
will need time to dry before placing them on the cupcakes.

Roll out white vanilla fondant until about one-eighth of an
inch thick, then print and use Gallifreyan Symbol template
to create a fondat topper, according to instructions on page
204. (Visit books.geeksweets.net to print template.) You can
also use a round cookie cutter or the top of a glass that is
close in size to the circle in the template.

Place a printed, cut-out Gallifreyan symbol of your choice
on top of one of the fondant circles, lining up the edges.
Using a pen or pencil, trace the symbol onto the fondant
by pressing just hard enough to make indentations in the
fondant through the paper. (Be careful not to press so hard
that you tear through the paper!)

Using a black edible ink pen, trace the indentations to
create your Gallifreyan symbols *(Figure 1)*.

(Figure 1)

Set aside and allow symbol toppers to harden.

Preheat oven to 350° F; line cupcake tins with cupcake liners.

Mix room temperature cream cheese, lightly beaten egg, and one-third cup of sugar in a small bowl. Stir in chocolate chips and set aside.

Mix the remaining ingredients for the black bottoms together with a stand or hand mixer.

Fill cupcake liners one-third to one-half of the way to the top with the black bottom mixture using a disher or spoon. Drop a large spoonful of the cream cheese mixture on top of each cupcake until two-thirds full (Figure 2).

Bake 20-25 minutes until centers are set. Carefully remove from the cupcake pan and allow to come to room temperature.

While cupcakes are cooling, prepare the Classic Buttercream recipe (see page 58) with one tablespoon of vanilla flavoring.

(Figure 2)

Divide the buttercream into three equal portions. You can use a kitchen scale if you have one, or just eyeball it. Dye one-third of the buttercream purple, one-third blue, and the last third teal. (Don't have teal dye? You can use the blue with a hint of green for the same effect.)

Create a 3-color piping bag with the directions from page 31 (Figures 3 and 4).

(Figure 3)

(Figure 4)

When cupcakes are cooled, frost a **classic rosette** with the 3-color piping bag fitted with a large star tip. (See page 28 for frosting techniques.)

(Figure 5)

Immediately after frosting each cupcake, while the frosting is still wet, sprinkle with the white sprinkles to make the stars in the galaxy. Ooooo, pretty *(Figure 5)*.

Lastly, top with Gallifreyan symbol toppers. **Note:** toppers will begin to soften and wilt a couple of hours after adding to moist buttercream, so only add to top of cupcakes shortly before serving.

Now have all your Time Lord buddies over for a big family reunion potluck! (What's that you say? There's only the one out there? ...oh. Well, they'll keep in the freezer until Gallifrey surfaces again.)

SKILL CHECK:

Want to compose your own Gallifreyan love letters or Intergalactic Yelp reviews? Visit https://adrian17.github.io/Gallifreyan/ and use Adrian Wielgosik's amazing Gallifreyan online translation device to write your own custom topper messages.

QUEST REQUIREMENTS:

*Foolproof Vanilla Cupcakes recipe
(see page 42)*

*Classic Buttercream recipe
(see page 58)*

1 tablespoon vanilla

Zest of 1 lemon

Zest of 2 limes

3-inch ball chocolate fondant

*Gel food coloring
(black, blue, orange)*

Portal Cupcakes template

*Cupcake liners
(black recommended)*

1 piping bag with large round tip

*2 piping bags with
medium star tips*

X-acto knife

Waxed paper

PORTAL CUPCAKES

If you're looking to get experimental but you've misplaced your Aperture Science Handheld Portal Device, you can still simulate the experiment by creating inter-spatial portals across the top of two cupcakes. These cupcakes are infused with a bright hit of citrus to help keep your subjects alert and in top puzzle-solving condition...and this experiment actually will end with cake!

MAKES **22-25 QUANTUM TUNNELING HUBS**

Make fondant "research participants" ahead of time, or even a day before, as they will need time to dry before placing them on the cupcakes.

Tint chocolate fondant black with gel food coloring and roll out until about one-eighth of an inch thick, then print and use Portal Cupcakes template, according to instructions on page 204. (Visit books.geeksweets.net to print template.)

Preheat oven to 350° F; line cupcake tins with cupcake liners.

Prepare the Foolproof Vanilla Cupcakes recipe to the point when batter is complete (see page 42), then divide the batter into two equal portions.

Mix the zest of one lemon into one-half of the batter and use it to fill the orange liners. Mix the zest of two limes into the remaining batter and use it to fill the blue cupcake liners. Liners should be filled two-thirds of the way full using a disher or spoon.

Bake 15-20 minutes, until a wooden toothpick inserted into the center of the cupcake comes out clean. Carefully remove from the cupcake pan and allow to come to room temperature.

While cupcakes are cooling, prepare the Classic Buttercream recipe (see page 58) with one tablespoon of vanilla. Split the buttercream into three portions, with one portion being a bit larger the other two.

Add the juice of one lemon to one of the smaller portions and dye with orange gel food coloring. Fill a piping bag outfitted with a medium star tip.

Add the juice of two limes to the other of the smaller portions and dye with blue gel food coloring. Fill a piping bag outfitted with a medium star tip.

Fill another piping bag with a large round tip with the final, uncolored larger portion of frosting.

Frost a **flat top** on the cupcakes with the white buttercream first, just a thin layer, right to the edge of the cupcake *(Figure 1)*. See page 28 for frosting techniques.

Frost a round blue portal on the cupcakes in the blue liners, and an orange portal on the cupcakes in the orange liners *(Figure 2)*.

(Figure 1)

(Figure 2)

Place your dudes into the cupcakes so that they appear to be jumping into an orange portal cupcake, then coming out of a blue portal cupcake. The template makes the torso a bit longer in order to have something to press down deep into the cupcake.

Now you're thinking with portals!

SKILL CHECK:

The little fondant dudes will start to wilt after a couple of hours, perhaps buckling under the rigorous pressures of everyday laboratory life, or perhaps because they're made out of sugar, so place them in the cupcakes right before serving to keep them perky and ready to go. If you have leftovers, you can pull them out of the cupcakes and place them on a sheet of waxed paper to firm them back up.

SIDE QUEST

PARTYIN' IN THE GALAXY

That's another level of training down, adventurer! Congrats! Before you set your sights on slaying the dragons in the next level, it's time for an interstellar vacay through the galaxy. And who better to adventure through the galaxy with than the very Guardians sworn to protect it. Sure, one's a tree, the big guy never gets your jokes, and the little trash panda lookin' one keeps giving you the stink eye, but otherwise, these guys seem swell and their party soundtrack is rad. WE ARE GROOT!

Visit books.geeksweets.net to print your own 'Partyin' in the Galaxy' invites!

QUEST REQUIREMENTS:

9 cups Captain Crunch cereal

1 cup milk chocolate chips

4 tablespoons butter

½ cup smooth peanut butter

2 cups icing sugar

1 cup Reese's Pieces

1 cup mini marshmallows

1 gallon-sized resealable freezer
bag (or large tupperware with lid)

Medium resealable plastic bags

Rocket Fuel printable tags

ROCKET FUEL

You gotta fuel up to keep up. These Guardians know how to party! Grab a bag of Rocket Fuel and let the sugar rush get you through another round of "Oooga Chaka" hip shaking.

"I can't stop this feee-liiin', deep insiiide of me..."

MAKES **12-14 CUPS / SERVINGS**

Melt milk chocolate chips and butter together in the microwave in 15 second bursts, stirring between each interval, until chips are melted and butter is incorporated.

Remove from microwave and stir in peanut butter.

Place cereal in a large bowl and pour chocolate peanut butter mixture over the top. Gently stir until cereal is completely coated on all sides *(Figure 1)*.

Add chocolate covered cereal mixture to large freezer bag or tupperware along with icing sugar. Seal bag or attach lid and shake until mixture is completely covered, breaking up any large chunks as you go *(Figure 2)*.

(Figure 1)

(Figure 2)

Once cooled, add in Reese's Pieces and mini marshmallows and mix until combined. Add one cup to each medium-sized resealable bag.

Print as many Rocket Fuel printable tags as required. (Visit books.geeksweets.net for printables.) Fold over in the middle, and using a stapler, attach to the top of the bags.

QUEST REQUIREMENTS:

2 cups chocolate milk

4 cups root beer
(or more, depending on glass size)

8 scoops chocolate ice cream

4 scoops mint chocolate ice cream

½ cup chocolate syrup /
ice cream topping

Aerosol whipped cream

4 mint sprigs (optional)

4 large mugs or glasses, chilled

Green straws (optional)

GROOT BEER FLOAT

*"WE. ARE… ABOUT TO DRINK AN AMAZING
ROOT BEER FLOAT!"*

MAKES **4 FLOATS**

Using a spoon or directly from the bottle, drizzle a few thin lines of chocolate syrup on the inside of four tall see-through glasses. Don't use too much, or you won't be able to see the tasty goings-on inside the glasses.

Pour half a cup of chocolate milk into each glass. Add one cup of root beer (or enough to fill the glass just over halfway).

Add two scoops of chocolate ice cream and top with one scoop of mint chocolate ice cream. (Fill to top with additional root beer if glass is not full.)

Top with a heaping spiral of whipped cream and a mint sprig.

The handsome one nudges your elbow and passes you a flask. You twist off the top and smell sweet vanilla over some kind of alcohol that makes your eyes water. "The big guy is going to start Karaoke soon." he says. "You might need some of this before we begin. He's big into Manilow."

For a more adult version of this beverage, add two ounces of vanilla vodka when pouring in the root beer.

DRAGON SLAYER

"Epic recipes and skill checks for the most heroic of bakers."

UNICORN POOP COOKIES

The majestic unicorn is an elusive beast, known for its beautiful silken mane, mighty opal horn, and of course, its delicious droppings! (Hey, don't knock it 'till you try it.) The best method is to corral one into your kitchen, feed it lots of cupcakes, then patiently wait for its glittery payload. Can't find a unicorn in your neck of the woods, adventurer? Follow the instructions below to craft your very own "unicorn poops" and impress/gross out your friends!

QUEST REQUIREMENTS:

1 batch No-Fail Sugar Cookie recipe from page 72, made with 4 ½ cups of sugar instead of 5.

Wilton gel food coloring in rose, orange, golden yellow, teal, and violet

¼ cup white (clear) corn syrup

2 tablespoons Disco Dust (edible, non-toxic glitter)

Stand or hand mixer

Plastic or latex gloves

Kitchen scale

Cookie sheet

Drying rack

Large soft paintbrush

MAKES **16 LARGE POOPS**

Preheat oven to 350° F.

Prepare one batch of the No-Fail Sugar Cookie recipe from page 72. Make sure to use 4 ½ cups of sugar instead of the 5 cups the recipe calls for.

Once dough is complete, weigh entire batch on kitchen scale *(Figure 1)*. Divide that number by 5, and use kitchen scale to separate out into five balls of equal weight *(Figure 2)*.

(Figure 1)

(Figure 2)

SKILL CHECK:

While you can eyeball your portions, you will have more uniform results using a kitchen scale to separate everything out. But don't sweat it if you don't have a scale – these <u>are</u> poops we're talking about here.

Wearing gloves to protect your hands from the dye, dye each ball into the five specified colors - rose, orange, golden yellow, teal, and violet *(Figures 3 and 4)*. These color names refer to specific Wilton branded gel food dyes to achieve the colors shown here, but feel free to mix your own, or even change up the colors to whatever you like! But do make sure you are using gel dyes, and not the liquid dyes you find at the supermarket. (To learn more about the differences in dyes, turn to page 19.)

(Figure 3)

(Figure 4)

Separate out each dyed ball into 20 equal smaller balls, one color for each of the 20 cookies, using the kitchen scale. (They will be in the ballpark of 0.75 / 20g per ball.) Leave them on a tray covered in plastic wrap while you create each cookie, otherwise they will develop a dry crust on the outside of the balls that will cause the cookies to crack.

Working with one ball of each color, roll balls into round sticks about 3.5 inches long *(Figure 5)*. Press the sticks together with rose, orange, and yellow on the bottom and teal and violet on top *(Figure 6)*.

(Figure 5)

(Figure 6)

Starting at the middle and then rolling outwards to push out any air bubbles, begin rolling the sticks together with your fingers *(Figure 7)*. Continue rolling outwards until you have a roll that is 12-15 inches long with tapered ends. If you roll one end up while rolling the other one down, you will twist the dough into a swirl of color that will make a cookie that shows off all colors involved *(Figure 8)*.

(Figure 7)

(Figure 8)

Carefully lifting up the rainbow roll without breaking it, coil it on top of itself four to five times. Make it as tall as possible as it will flatten out when baked *(Figures 9 and 10).* Place a maximum of six cookies per cookie sheet, so they do not touch when they spread out.

(Figure 9)

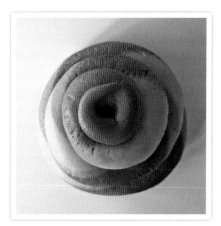

(Figure 10)

Place cookie sheet in freezer for 15 minutes until cookie coils are firm and chilled through. (This will make it so they flatten more slowly during the baking process, which will help them hold more of their shape.)

Bake 22-25 minutes in preheated oven, or until edges of cookies begin to brown. (Do not undercook – cookies are quite thick and will likely need the full amount of time to begin to brown.)

While cookies are cooling, mix one-quarter cup of corn syrup with one-eighth of a cup warm water until combined.

Remove cooled cookies from cookie sheet and place on waxed paper. (Don't forget this step, as we're about to get glittery, and it can get EVERYWHERE.)

Going one cookie at a time, use a paint or pastry brush to paint the surface of the cookie with the corn syrup mixture until glossy *(Figure 11)*.

Using a large soft paintbrush, dip into the disco dust or non-toxic glitter and tap the brush over the cookie, raining glitter down onto the sticky surface *(Figure 12)*. Just a small tap will do, a little goes a long way!

(Figure 11)

(Figure 12)

Allow poops to dry, then place in a container between sheets of waxed paper. They can be stored in a cool dry place for up to a week, or in the freezer for up to two months.

QUEST REQUIREMENTS:

Red Velvet Cupcakes recipe
(see page 46)

Cream Cheese Frosting recipe
(see page 64)

5-inch ball chocolate or
black fondant

5-inch ball white (or red fondant
with a small amount of white)

Red and black gel food coloring
(if not using pre-dyed fondant)

Edible ink printer and frosting
sheet (optional)

Heart Container template

Wax paper

Small paring or X-acto knife

Piping bag fitted with large star tip

Medium paintbrush

Cupcake liners (red recommended)

IT'S DANGEROUS TO GO ALONE, TAKE THESE RED VELVET CUPCAKES

Toppers for these cupcakes can be made in two ways – using the Custom Edible Toppers technique outlined on page 204, or with a piece of special equipment, purchased from the secret baking wizardry corners of the internet – an edible ink printer.

MAKES **22-24 HEART CONTAINER CUPCAKES**

Create heart container toppers: Make toppers ahead of time or even a day before, as they will need time to dry before placing them on the cupcakes.

If you have an edible ink printer, print the second page of the template out at 100% scale and store in a large plastic bag until ready to use. (Frosting sheets will dry out if left in the open air.)

Wearing gloves to protect your hands, dye chocolate fondant black and dye white fondant red, reserving a small amount of white. If you have fondant that is already dyed, skip ahead to the next step. (If you are using the edible ink printer method, only dye the black fondant.)

Roll each fondant color out until about one-eighth of an inch thick, then print and use the Heart container template, according to instructions on page 204 *(Figures 1 and 2).* Visit books.geeksweets.net to print templates.

(Figure 1)

(Figure 2)

Note: If you are using an edible ink printer, you will only need to cut the largest heart template out of the black

---

fondant. If not, cut the large heart size in black, and the small heart size in red, as well as the small white square.

If using edible ink printer, cut out hearts from frosting sheet with small scissors or an X-acto knife.

With a paintbrush or your finger, paint a small amount of water onto the surface of the black fondant piece. Attach edible ink printer heart and press down with paper towel, being careful not to smudge the ink. If not using printed hearts, instead attach red fondant heart and white highlight square. Allow toppers to dry completely overnight.

Preheat oven to 350° F; line cupcake tins with cupcake liners. Prepare the Red Velvet Cupcakes recipe (see page 46).

(Figure 3)

Fill cupcake liners two-thirds of the way to the top with a disher or spoon. Bake 20 minutes, or until a wooden toothpick inserted into the center of the cupcake comes out clean. Carefully remove from the cupcake pan and allow to come to room temperature. While cupcakes are cooling, prepare the Cream Cheese Frosting recipe (see page 64).

Fill piping bag and frost a **classic rosette** onto cupcakes with large star tip, (see page 28 for frosting techniques). Top with Heart Container toppers. **Note:** toppers will begin to soften and wilt a couple of hours after adding to moist buttercream, so only place on cupcakes shortly before serving.

Expansion Pack: Included in the template are two images to print and present with the cupcakes if you are giving them as a gift. Place the first image of the wizard on the outside of the box or tupperware, and the second image on the inside.

(Figure 4)

SKILL CHECK:

Interested in making your toppers using an edible ink printer, but don't want to drop the gold on the required equipment? Try using that high-level charisma of yours to sweet-talk a grocery store bakery into printing a sheet for you. Most have one for making photo cakes, and some will let you print a sheet for a small fee – just bring the provided PDF heart template with you on a USB stick, and have them print the page of hearts.

— LEVEL 3 —
DRAGON SLAYER

QUEST REQUIREMENTS:

*Foolproof Vanilla Cupcakes recipe
(see page 42)*

*Classic Buttercream recipe
(see page 58)*

*Candy melts, ½ cup each color
(pink, orange, yellow, blue)*

Candy melts, 1 cup purple.

3-inch ball white fondant

*Gel food coloring (no-taste red,
pink, orange, yellow, teal, green,
blue, and purple)*

Blue edible ink pen

White star sprinkles

Vanilla flavoring

*Assorted flavoring oils as desired
(I used apple, lemon, grape,
bubble gum, and tropical punch)*

3 piping bags with large round tips

1 piping bag with large star tip

*10 intact piping bags with no
tips cut off (for multicolor frosting
technique and candy melts)*

*Cupcake liners (pink, orange,
yellow, blue, and purple)*

Stand or hand mixer

Tweezers (optional)

CUTIE MARK CUPCAKES

*This baking challenge will test your fondant shaping skills,
requiring you to create intricate edible pieces of art to go
on top of these multi-flavor, multi-color, multi-awesome
delights, straight from Equestria.*

But it's totes worth it, right, because ERMAGHERD, PONIES!

MAKES **22-25 CUTIE CUPCAKES**

Preheat oven to 350° F.

While oven is preheating, create the fondant toppers as
shown below *(Figures 1 through 6)*. Fondant will need to be
dyed as required using instructions found on page 33.

(Figure 1)

(Figure 2)

(Figure 3)

(Figure 4)

(Figure 5)   (Figure 6)

Prepare the Foolproof Vanilla Cupcakes recipe to the point when batter is complete (see page 42) with two teaspoons vanilla flavoring.

Separate the batter out into six equal parts in separate bowls. I use a kitchen scale to do this accurately, but you can easily just eyeball it or use an ice cream scoop, disher, or spoon.

Dye and flavor the separated batter as follows:

- ✦ One portion with orange dye and apple flavoring
- ✦ One portion with yellow dye and lemon flavoring
- ✦ One portion with purple dye and grape flavoring
- ✦ One portion with pink dye and bubble gum flavoring
- ✦ One portion with blue dye and tropical punch flavoring
- ✦ One portion left as is, with no dye and only the vanilla flavoring added when making the batter recipe

Use four of each color cupcake liner to line cupcake pans as follows:

- ✦ 4 pink liners for the pink dyed batter
- ✦ 4 orange liners for the orange dyed batter
- ✦ 4 yellow liners for the yellow dyed batter
- ✦ 4 blue liners for the blue dyed batter
- ✦ 4 purple liners for the purple dyed batter
- ✦ 4 purple liners for the batter with no dye added

Fill cupcake liners two-thirds of the way to the top with a disher or spoon, according to the colors listed above. Bake 15-20 minutes, until a wooden toothpick inserted into the center of a cupcake comes out clean. Carefully remove from the cupcake pan and allow to come to room temperature.

While cupcakes are cooling, prepare the Classic Buttercream recipe (see page 58), with two tablespoons of vanilla flavoring.

Separate the frosting out into six equal parts in separate bowls. (Again, use a kitchen scale for accuracy, or feel free to just eyeball it.)

Dye and flavor the separated frosting as follows:

- ✦ One portion with yellow dye and apple flavoring
- ✦ Three portions with pink dye and no flavoring
- ✦ One portion with no dye and vanilla flavoring
- ✦ The last portion will be used to make the rainbow swirl frosting in the next step!

Make the rainbow piping bag: Take the non-dyed portion from the last step and separate it out into five portions. Dye each portion as follows: 1 pink, 1 orange, 1 yellow, 1 teal, and 1 purple. With these five portions, create a single multicolor piping bag by following the instructions on page 31.

Fill the remaining piping bags with other dyed frostings. All piping bags should have a large round tip, with the rainbow piping bag being the only one with a large star tip.

Frost cupcakes, (following the frosting techniques on page 28) as follows:

- ✦ 4 pink liners with the pink batter – frost **flat top** with pink frosting
- ✦ 4 orange liners with the orange batter – frost **flat top** with yellow frosting
- ✦ 4 yellow liners with the yellow batter – frost **flat top** with pink frosting
- ✦ 4 blue liners with the blue batter – frost **classic rosette** with rainbow piping bag
- ✦ 4 purple liners with purple batter – frost **flat top** with pink frosting
- ✦ 4 purple liners with batter with no dye added - frost **flat top** with frosting with no dye

Add each of the candy melt colors to the remaining intact piping bags as follows:

- ✦ 1 bag pink, 1 bag orange, 1 bag yellow, 1 bag blue
- ✦ 1 bag purple (this one is larger, as it will be used to melt chocolate over 8 cupcakes, while the others will only melt chocolate over 4.)

Twist bags closed, sealing with an elastic. Place each in microwave and heat briefly until just melted, about 30 seconds to a minute. (Purple will take longer as it will be a bigger bag.)

Cut one-quarter inch off the tip of each bag of melted candy melts. (You can sit them upside down in drinking glasses to stop the melted chocolate from oozing out!) Drizzle blobs of melted candy melt on top of each cupcake as noted in the color pairings below, using just enough so it still shows the frosting color under the candy melts and does not run down the side of the cupcake.

Note: As you pour the candy melt on each cupcake, add the corresponding fondant topper to each one before the candy melt dries, pressing down gently to embed the fondant pieces into the candy melt *(Figures 7 to 12)*. You can use a clean pair of tweezers to add the tiny elements, like the white star sprinkles.

(Figure 7)

(Figure 8)

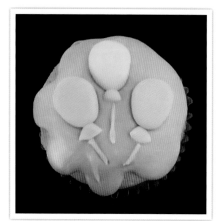

(Figure 9)

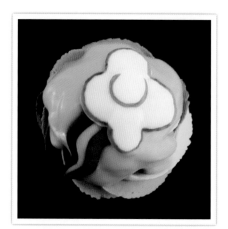

(Figure 10)

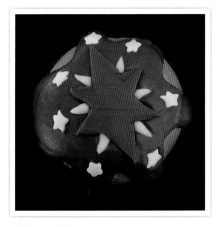

(Figure 11)   (Figure 12)

The color pairings are as follows:

- ✦ 4 pink liners with pink batter and pink frosting – pink candy melt and balloon fondant pieces

- ✦ 4 orange liners with orange batter and yellow frosting – orange candy melt with apple fondant pieces

- ✦ 4 yellow liners with yellow batter and pink frosting – yellow candy melt with butterfly fondant pieces

- ✦ 4 blue liners with blue batter and rainbow frosting – blue candy melt with lightning bolt fondant pieces

- ✦ 4 purple liners with purple batter and pink frosting – purple candy melt with starburst fondant pieces and white star sprinkles

- ✦ 4 purple liners with batter and frosting with no dye added – purple candy melt with blue star fondant pieces

Allow candy melt to fully dry before serving or storing cupcakes (or even letting them bump into each other!)

SKILL CHECK:

If you can't track down all the baking cup colors recommended, no worries! You can just use white liners, and the color of the dye in the cupcake batter will show through once baked.

QUEST REQUIREMENTS:

Cake pop recipe (see page 52 for recipe and supplies)

1 package white chocolate candy melts

½ cup black candy melts

White jimmies (the tiny cylindrical kind of sprinkles)

Assorted sprinkles and candies resembling sushi roll insides

1 intact piping bag

Toothpicks

Tweezers (optional)

SKILL CHECK:

Smaller candies and sprinkles work best on top of these cake pops, so raid your favorite candy store and use your imagination to recreate your favorite sushi roll flavors and ingredients. For these, I used orange candy-coated chocolate chips as fish roe, green shamrock sprinkles as lettuce, and green spider candies cut in half to serve as the avocado.

SUSHI CAKE POPS

What's better than a big plate of delicious sushi rolls? A big plate of sushi rolls that are actually made of cake and chocolate! Have sushi for dessert with these sneaky swap-in sweets by following the directions below.

MAKES **40-50 SUSHI ROLLS ON STICKS**

Follow cake pop recipe from page 52, right up until the pops are ready to shape.

Roll an oval shape instead of a circle, then using a flat surface, flatten out the top and bottom of the ball until it resembles a sushi roll shape *(Figures 1 and 2)*.

(Figure 1)

(Figure 2)

Melt white candy melts and attach cake shape to the lollipop stick as directed in the cake pop recipe on page 55.

Dip pop in melted white candy melts, and while the chocolate is still wet, hold over a large bowl and sprinkle handfuls of white sprinkles over the pop, letting the excess fall back into the bowl. Rotate pop as you are pouring to cover all sides *(Figure 3)*.

Chocolate will harden fast, so only do one pop at a time. If you find a few gaps, use a toothpick to smear on additional melted chocolate and a pair of tweezers to fill in the gaps with the white sprinkles. You can also roll the pop in your hand to help distribute the sprinkles *(Figure 4)*.

(Figure 3)

(Figure 4)

While sprinkled pops are drying, add one cup black candy melts to a piping bag with no tip and twist closed, sealing with an elastic. Place in microwave and heat briefly until just melted, about 30 seconds to a minute.

Snip off the tip of the piping bag and pipe a thin circle of black on the very top of the pop to represent the ring of seaweed in the sushi. Allow to dry *(Figure 5)*.

Using an assortment of candies and sprinkles, "fill" your sushi roll inside the black circle. Use a toothpick dipped in melted white candy melt and tweezers to help attach items *(Figure 6)*.

(Figure 5)

(Figure 6)

QUEST REQUIREMENTS:

Moist Chocolate Cupcake recipe
(see page 44)

Dark Chocolate Frosting recipe
(see page 62)

2 cups white chocolate candy melts

Gold luster dust

Gold food color spray

3-inch ball vanilla fondant

Green gel food coloring

Gold dragées

For Chocolate Mousse Filling:

3.5 oz (100g) bittersweet
chocolate, coarsely chopped

1 cup heavy cream

2 tablespoons granulated sugar

Skull chocolate mold

1 piping bag fitted with a medium
star tip, 2 piping bags with
tips still intact

Cupcake liners (brown or
gold recommended)

Double boiler, or a mixer bowl set
over a pan of simmering water

Clean, soft-bristled paintbrush

Small rolling pin

Cupcake corer (optional)

Chocolate handling gloves
(optional, but recommended)

DEATH BY CHOCOLATE CUPCAKES

Moist Devil's Food Chocolate cake, filled with sinful chocolate mousse, topped with dark chocolate frosting and a solid white chocolate skull and roses – truly a killer combo for chocolate lovers.

Having won the Ottawa Capital Cupcake Camp 2010 and featured in SKULL STYLE: Skulls in Contemporary Art and Design by Patrice Farameh in 2011, this cupcake has a pedigree and is not afraid to flaunt it. Bring this beauty out at your next RPG night to set the tone for a macabre tale.

MAKES **30-32 DEADLY DELISH CUPCAKES**

Preheat oven to 350° F; line cupcake tins with cupcake liners.

Create the chocolate mousse filling:

In a small heatproof bowl set over a saucepan of simmering water, heat one-quarter cup of the cream, stirring often, until steaming.

Remove bowl from pan and stir in chocolate until melted and smooth. (You can reheat it over the pan of hot water if the chocolate doesn't all melt – but be careful not to overheat!)

In a chilled bowl of an electric mixer, whip remaining cream until soft peaks form. Slowly add in sugar and vanilla extract until stiff peaks have just begun to form. (Stiff peaks are when you lift out the whisk attachment and the cream on the end of it comes to a point without folding over on itself.)

Fold one-quarter of the whipped cream into the cooled chocolate mixture, then fold that mixture back into the remaining whipped cream, stirring just until incorporated.

Add the mousse mixture to the two piping bags with the tips still attached and refrigerate for at least two hours.

Create the white chocolate skulls:

Add one cup white chocolate candy melts to a piping bag with no tip and twist closed, sealing with an elastic. Place in microwave and heat briefly until just melted, about 30 seconds to a minute.

Snip off the very tip of the piping bag and pipe the chocolate into skull chocolate mold until level *(Figure 1)*. Tap chocolate mold on a flat countertop to bring any bubbles to the surface.

Place full skull mold into the fridge on a level surface until set, 15 to 20 minutes. Remove from fridge and tap upside down on a countertop to release molded chocolate skull halves *(Figure 2)*.

Pipe a small amount of the white chocolate between the two halves and quickly press them together *(Figure 3)*. Wipe off any extra chocolate that oozes out the sides with a paper towel and use the excess chocolate to fill any gaps there may be between the two halves *(Figure 4)*.

(Figure 1)

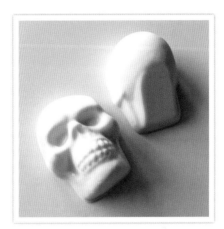

(Figure 2)

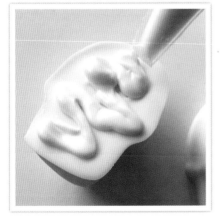

(Figure 3)

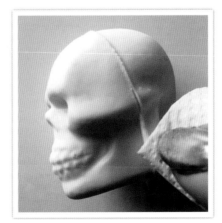

(Figure 4)

Put completed skulls back in the fridge for 10-15 minutes, then take them out and bring back to room temperature. As the chocolate cools, it will develop a thin layer of condensation on the surface. When it does, brush skulls with gold luster dust using a soft-bristled paintbrush. You can wear chocolate handling gloves to minimize the number of fingerprints you leave on the chocolate *(Figures 5 and 6)*.

(Figure 5)

(Figure 6)

Create the fondant roses:

Roll a small piece of vanilla fondant into a long oval, and roll up, pinching together at the middle to create two rose shapes *(Figures 7, 8 and 9)*. Brush with luster dust *(Figure 10)*. Create enough roses so you have three for each cupcake.

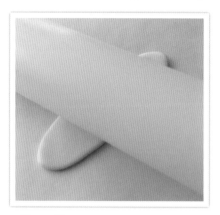

(Figure 7)

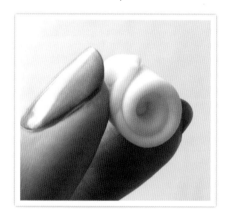

(Figure 8)

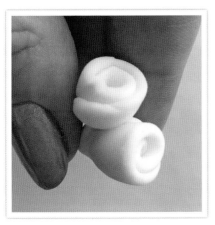

(Figure 9)

(Figure 10)

Dye a small amount of fondant green following instructions on page 33, and shape two leaves for each cupcake by rolling out a small oval with pointed ends, pinching it in the middle, then cutting it in half with a knife *(Figure 11)*.

Connect three roses and two leaves together with a tiny amount of water. Brush roses with gold luster dust and set aside to dry *(Figure 12)*.

(Figure 11)

(Figure 12)

Prepare the Moist Chocolate Cupcake recipe (see page 44).

Fill cupcake liners two-thirds of the way to the top with a disher or spoon. Bake 15-20 minutes, until a wooden toothpick inserted into the center of the cupcake comes out clean. Carefully remove from the cupcake pan and allow to come to room temperature.

When cupcakes are cooled, use a knife or a cupcake corer to remove a small amount of cake from the center of the cupcake. Feel free to nom immediately, or put in a ziplock bag in the freezer for future cake pops. (See page 52).

Remove piping bags with chocolate mousse from fridge and cut off tips. Pipe mousse into holes created in cupcakes.

Prepare the Rich Dark Chocolate Frosting recipe (see page 62).

The next steps will need to be done quickly, one cupcake at a time, as the frosting will begin to set, making it difficult to add the toppers.

Frost a **flat rosette** with a piping bag fitted with a medium star tip. (See page 28 for frosting techniques.)

Spray with gold food color spray. Spraying a light dusting at a low angle while rotating the cupcake will give a nice "gilded edge" effect.

Top with white chocolate skull, roses and a few gold dragées. (If frosting has started to harden, pop the cupcake in the microwave for a few seconds to re-soften it.)

SKILL CHECK:

This recipe uses an eggless version of classic chocolate mousse, but feel free to use your own recipe or the "ain't nobody got time for that" option of boxed chocolate mousse from the grocery store. Because of the mousse inside the cupcakes – it is perishable, and they should be stored in tupperware in the fridge until ready to eat. Allow to come to room temperature 30 minutes to an hour before serving.

QUEST REQUIREMENTS:

1 bag dark or milk chocolate candy melts

Gold luster dust

Han Solo 'Frozen in Carbonite' food-safe silicone ice cube tray

Small plastic microwavable cup or bowl

Small paintbrush

Large soft paintbrush

Plastic bags (optional)

Frozen in Carbon-bite bag toppers (optional)

For Mix-ins:

Salted Caramel Pretzel (Skor bits, chopped pretzels and sea salt)

*PB & Banana
(Chopped banana chips and chopped peanut butter cups)*

Mr. Munchy (Rice Krispies)

Cranberry Almond (Chopped Craisins and chopped almonds)

*Cashew Coconut
(Chopped cashews and shredded sweetened coconut)*

FROZEN IN CARBON-BITE CHOCOLATE BARS

Trade up liquid carbonite for tasty chocolate filled with goodies, and recreate everyone's favorite smuggler's darkest day... then eat him!

MAKES **6-7 CHOCOLATE BARS**

Prepare any "mix-in" ingredients in advance. (Chop nuts, break up pretzels, etc.) Use any of the flavor ideas listed, or come up with your own awesome flavor combinations!

Add one cup candy melts to a plastic microwave-safe bowl or cup and microwave in 30 second intervals until just melted, stirring after each interval; it should be warm, but not burning hot.

Make sure silicone mold is completely clean and dry.

Using a small paintbrush dipped in melted candy melts, thickly paint in face, hands, and feet of silicone mold, making sure to get all the way into the tiny details with no air bubbles *(Figure 1)*. Do this quickly, before the candy melt begins to dry.

Pour chocolate from the bowl into the candy mold, filling it three-quarters of the way to the top *(Figure 2)*.

(Figure 1)   *(Figure 2)*

Carefully lift up the filled tray, and while keeping it level, tap on a flat surface to allow chocolate to settle and make any air bubbles rise to the top. Continue to work quickly so the chocolate does not set.

While the chocolate is still melted, press in any mix-ins until the chocolate level has reached the top of the tray. Pat down evenly with your palm. Be careful not to press down so deep that your mix-ins reach the bottom of the tray *(Figures 3 and 4)*.

(Figure 3)

(Figure 4)

Place tray in freezer for at least 20 minutes until chocolate is completely hardened.

Once hardened, carefully remove by bending silicone mold to release, starting by pulling away the edges. If chocolate is completely hardened, the chocolate bar should come away easily. You can wear chocolate handling gloves or use a piece of paper towel to help minimize the amount of fingerprints on the surface of the chocolate.

(Figure 5)

(Figure 6)

While some condensation is still on the chilled chocolate bar, brush on a small amount of the gold luster dust, using a soft paintbrush *(Figures 5 and 6)*.

Repeat until you have used up all the remaining candy melts (or until you've got as many chocolate bars as you can handle). If your bowl of candy melts begins to harden on the edges, remelt in the microwave in 30 second bursts.

If packaging, allow chocolate to cool completely before adding to plastic bag. Print, cut, and fold bag topper and staple to top of plastic bag. Visit books. geeksweets.net for printables. Using a marker, label the flavors on the back of the tag *(Figures 7 and 8)*.

(Figure 7)

(Figure 8)

SKILL CHECK:

Candy melts are my chocolate of choice for these bars, as they are simple to work with and will not produce the white 'bloom' on the surface that chocolate chips or improperly tempered chocolate will produce. They won't, however, have the same 'snap' as tempered chocolate. I have not gone into detail on the process of tempering chocolate, but if this is a baking magic you have already mastered, then go ahead and use tempered chocolate instead of the candy melts for a more fancy-pants bar.

— LEVEL 3 —
DRAGON SLAYER

QUEST REQUIREMENTS:

1 cup plus 2 tablespoons salted
butter, browned (see instructions)

1 ¼ cups granulated sugar

1 cup brown sugar

3 cups cake flour (not all-purpose)

2 teaspoons cinnamon

1 ½ cups all-purpose flour

¾ teaspoon baking soda

2 ¼ teaspoons baking powder

1 ½ teaspoons salt

5 large whole eggs plus 3 egg
yolks, room temperature

2 cups buttermilk,
room temperature

1 teaspoon vanilla

1 teaspoon butter flavoring

4-inch ball of vanilla fondant

2-inch ball of chocolate fondant

Gel food coloring in black, red,
and yellow

CONTINUED ON PAGE 197

"YOU'RE A WIZARD, CUPCAKE!"

You don't have to be "the boy who lived" to enjoy all the flavors of the wizarding world's favorite beverage – just "the person who purchased this book." Described as a sickly-sweet butterscotch cream soda, this now-famous beverage translates perfectly into cupcakes.

This recipe includes the step of "burning your butter", which sounds like crazy talk, but is actually a great technique to use to give these cupcakes a unique flavor. So read the instructions below on how to brown your butter, then get all your quest items together, throw on your Gryffindor apron, and let's make some magic!

MAKES **25-30 LITTLE WIZARDS**

Cupcakes can be made with fondant pieces if you're feeling fancy, or just decorated with a drizzle of the butterscotch ice cream topping if you just want to get to shoving them in your face already. If making cupcakes with fondant toppings, prepare fondant elements as detailed below, letting pieces dry overnight. Scarves will need to stay soft in order to wrap around cupcake, so instead, place these inside a plastic bag with excess air removed until ready to use.

Dye half of the white fondant red and the other half yellow, wearing gloves to protect your hands from the dye. Set aside a small amount of red for the mouths, and a small amount of yellow for the lightning bolts.

Make scarves by rolling red and yellow tubes of fondant, setting them next to each other, and rolling out flat on a piece of waxed paper. Cut into striped strips *(Figures 1, 2 and 3)*.

(Figure 1)

(Figure 2)

something as expensive as
sent it?' said Hermione.
said Ron, impatiently. 'Listen, Harry, can I
ride that broom just yet.

QUEST REQUIREMENTS:

For the Frosting:

Classic Buttercream recipe
(see page 58)

8 tablespoons butterscotch ice
cream topping

1 teaspoon vanilla

1 teaspoon cream soda flavoring or
root beer flavoring

Wizard Glasses template

Piping bag with large star tip

Cupcake liners
(gold or brown recommended)

Cupcake corer (optional)

X-acto knife

Waxed paper

Tweezers

(Figure 3)

(Figure 4)

Cut fringe on either end of scarf and place in a plastic bag with the air removed so as not to dry out.

Wearing gloves to protect your hands from the dye, tint chocolate fondant black and roll out until about one-eighth of an inch thick. Print and use Wizard Glasses template, according to instructions on page 204. (Visit books. geeksweets.net to print template.) Allow glasses to dry until firm before adding to cupcakes, overnight is best.

With the remaining yellow fondant, roll out until one-eighth of an inch thick. Print and use Wizard Lightning Bolt template following the same procedure as for the Wizard Glasses. Allow to dry completely as well.

Roll two small balls of the remaining black fondant for the eyes, and slightly larger balls for the mouths. Slightly flatten both, and cut red ball in half with X-acto knife to complete mouth.

Store all pieces in open air overnight (except scarves!) to dry out.

Prepare the brown butter:

Cut up your cold butter and place it in a cold (not preheated) saucepan. Simmer over medium heat. The mixture will melt, then start foaming. Keep the heat as low as possible while still maintaining it at a simmer until your kitchen smells like pancakes.

Once the foam has turned brown, take it off the heat and allow it to cool for 10 minutes. (Don't let it go much longer or it can go from brown to black, and then it's icky. You want a nice amber color.)

Strain the butter by any effective means – with cheesecloth, coffee filter, or a fine mesh strainer into a bowl to remove any sediment. Let the butter solidify slightly before using. (This can take from a half hour to an hour depending on the temperature of your kitchen – don't stick it in the fridge!)

More than you've ever wanted to know about browned butter: Also called "beurre noisette," browned butter is the act of burning the milk solids in the butter, giving it a really rich and distinctive flavor. It's great in a lot of recipes, but I love it in cupcakes. Try it in place of oil in your next cake mix, or in some mashed potatoes.

Once butter has solidified but is still soft to the touch, preheat your oven to 350° F.

With your mixer on medium-high speed, cream browned butter and both types of sugar until pale and fluffy, about five minutes.

While butter and sugar is creaming, sift together both flours, baking soda, baking powder, cinnamon and salt in a large bowl.

Reduce speed to low and add whole eggs one at a time, beating until each is incorporated and scraping down sides of bowl as needed. Add yolks, and beat until thoroughly combined. Beat in vanilla and butter flavoring.

Add flour mixture in three batches, alternating with two additions of buttermilk and beating until just combined after each.

Fill cupcake liners two-thirds of the way to the top with a disher or spoon. Bake 16-18 minutes until a wooden toothpick inserted into the center of the cupcake comes out clean. Carefully remove from the cupcake pan and allow to come to room temperature.

While your cupcakes are cooling, prepare the Classic Buttercream recipe (see page 58). When complete, mix in butterscotch ice cream topping and cream soda or root beer flavoring to taste.

When cupcakes are cooled, use a knife or a cupcake corer to remove a small amount of cake from the center of the cupcake. Feel free to nom immediately, or put in a ziplock bag in the freezer for future cake pops. (See page 52).

Using a spoon, fill holes in cupcakes with a dollop of butterscotch ice cream topping.

Cupcakes can be frosted in a **tall coil** with a medium round tip, then drizzled with the butterscotch ice cream topping, OR if you've made the fondant pieces to resemble everyone's favorite lightning-scarred boy-wizard, frost cupcakes in a **classic rosette** with large star tip instead. (See page 28 for frosting techniques.)

Wrap scarf around base of frosting and dab with a dot of water to secure the scarf to itself. Add glasses, pressing into frosting to secure, then add eyes, mouth, and lightning bolt with a pair of tweezers to complete the face *(Figures 5 and 6)*.

(Figure 5)

(Figure 6)

QUEST REQUIREMENTS:

No-Fail Sugar Cookie recipe
(see page 72)

Royal Icing recipe (see page 70)

Gel food coloring
(black and no-taste red)

2-inch ball of white fondant

For Chocolate Ganache

8.8 oz (250g) heavy cream

7 oz (200g) bittersweet chocolate,
chopped into small pieces

1.2 oz (35g) salted butter at
room temperature

Merc in your Mouth template

Waxed paper

Rolling pin

Clean X-acto knife or sharp
paring knife

1 piping bag fitted with a #3 tip,
filled with red royal icing

1 piping bag fitted with
medium round tip

MERC IN YOUR MOUTH COOKIES

This antihero may be a bad influence on you, adventurer. I don't want you hanging out with him anymore. And no sleeping over at his place when his parents aren't home. No matter how good the breakfast chimichangas are.

MAKES **2-3 DOZEN COOKIE SANDWICHES**

Prepare the No-Fail Sugar Cookie recipe as directed on page 72 to the point when dough is complete. Chill.

Divide prepared chilled dough into two equal parts. With the first half, cut intact circles using the "Circle #1" shape from the Merc in your Mouth Cookie template and the cookie dough rolling / cutting instructions from page 35. (Visit books.geeksweets.net to print template.) Alternately, use a large round cookie cutter if you have one.

Cut the other half of the dough into the same large circle shapes. Using an X-acto knife and the "Circle #2" shape from the template, cut out the eyeholes. Alternately, you can use a smaller round cookie cutter to cut out the middle, then slice off the right and left sides of the smaller circle and add the line back to the middle of the large circle. This will create what can only be called a "Ghostbusters logo" shaped cookie *(Figures 1 and 2)*.

(Figure 1)

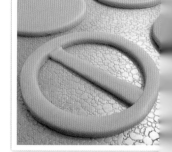

(Figure 2)

Bake cookies at 350° F for 8-10 minutes or until just beginning to turn brown around the edges. Carefully remove from baking sheet and allow to cool completely. (Be gentle!)

While cookies are cooling, prepare Royal Icing recipe from page 70 and dye bright red with no-taste red. (It will take quite a large amount of dye to get to a bright, strong red color, as opposed to how much it takes with most gel dye colors.) Fill piping bags as listed in the quest requirements, following the directions on page 27, and store in a sealed container, or a bowl covered with a wet cloth.

Lay down a base of waxed paper, then sit one of the cookies with the bar down the middle on top of a cookie cutter or drying rack. Coat the surface of the cookie with the red frosting by using a back and forth motion while squeezing the icing from the bag *(Figure 3)*. Allow the icing to drip down all sides of the cookie so it is completely covered *(Figure 4)*. Use a knife to remove any errant drips that do not fall off the cookie. Excess red icing can be scooped up off the waxed paper back into the piping bag as needed between cookies. Complete with remaining cookies and allow to dry completely, for at least an hour.

(Figure 3)

(Figure 4)

While cookies are drying, make the chocolate ganache: Use a kitchen scale to measure all ganache ingredients out in grams. Chop chocolate into very small pieces – try not to leave any large chunks! You can use a food processor if you have one. Set aside in a large bowl.

Boil cream in a heavy saucepan on the stove top. Allow to reach a boil for just a few seconds, then remove. Pour warmed cream onto chopped chocolate and let sit for two minutes. Blend with immersion blender, or whisk by hand until smooth. Once combined, add butter and whisk until smooth.

Cool ganache in the fridge until it has a thicker consistency that's good for piping from a piping bag. (Think 'room temperature butter'.) Check / stir every 10 minutes, as it can go from 'perfect consistency' to 'aww dang' quite quickly. If it does get too firm, allow the bowl to sit out at room temperature until it warms up a bit.

Dye completed ganache black by mixing in a small amount of black gel food dye – you'll only need a tiny bit.

Fill a piping bag fitted with a medium round tip with ganache, and pipe onto the "bottom" of the non-frosted cookies. (By "bottom" I mean the side that was face down on the cookie sheet when baking.) Starting at the outside edge, pipe a good layer of ganache in a swirl until you hit the middle of the cookie.

Take the dried, frosted red top of the cookie and sandwich the two sides together so there is ganache in between them.

Make the eyes: Roll fondant out on a piece of waxed paper to a thickness of about one-eighth of an inch, and cut eyes from the Merc with a Mouth template according to instructions on page 35. You will need two eyes for each cookie *(Figure 5)*.

Place eyes on top of cookie in the middle of the open sections and press down into ganache to hold in place *(Figure 6)*.

(Figure 5)   *(Figure 6)*

Cookies should be stored in the fridge for up to one week. (Do not stack them on top of each other, as the ganache will remain creamy and can rub off on other cookies.)

SKILL CHECK:

Chocolate Ganache IS. THE. BOMB. Melted on ice cream, smooshed between cookies, whipped into buttercream – you name it, ganache tastes good on it. While it can be a tricky magic to master, once you get the hang of it, you won't be able to stop making it. A common trip-up is leaving it in the fridge too long, which can make it too hard to pipe. If that happens, bring it to room temperature, or even melt it in the microwave slightly and start the fridge process again, this time watching it like a hawk or some other super-attentive bird.

QUEST REQUIREMENTS:

Fondant (chocolate for brown or
black, vanilla for all other colors.)

Gel food coloring

Solid vegetable shortening

Waxed paper

Rolling pin

Plastic (not silicone!) gloves

Clean X-acto knife or
sharp paring knife

Small detail paintbrush

Custom Cupcake Topper
template of choice
(visit books.geeksweets.net to for a
selection of printable templates)

CUSTOM EDIBLE TOPPERS

All right, Slayer of Dragons – you've done it. You've baked the cupcakes, crafted the cake pops, bested the cookies and saved a princess or two. Your baking prowess is now unmatched throughout the land, your mind is brimming with the profound principles of Magic Baking Dark Arts, and your hands are tainted by no-taste red gel dye and the blood of that one Orc Warrior King.

But this is it. Your greatest challenge yet. Custom Cupcake Toppers. The results are some awe-inspiring baked goods that people will come from far and wide to witness, crafted into the form of their favorite fandoms – made-to-order, and completely unique. Start with the provided templates, then let your imagination run wild!

Good luck, hero – we're counting on you.

Always begin your Custom Cupcake Toppers a day before, or even two if you can. They will require some time to dry out before assembling, and the drier they are, the longer they will stand up when placed on top of your cupcake. The moisture from the frosting will eventually cause the topper to start to wilt, so place your toppers on your cupcakes as close to when you are presenting or eating them as you can.

Choose your desired Custom Cupcake Topper template (or design your own!), and determine what colors of fondant you will need to create it. For this example, we will use the superhero symbol of everyone's favorite caped-crusader / man-bat, so we will need yellow and black.

Dye fondant as required in amounts needed for the number of toppers you will be making. Remember, the fondant will be rolled out thin, so you may need less than you think. However, it's best to err on the side of caution, adventurer, as it may be hard to remix a certain color to exactly the same shade, and any leftovers can be saved wrapped in plastic wrap in an airtight container. In this case, I will be dying half my fondant black and half my fondant yellow, as need equal amounts of each.

Place a ball of fondant on a piece of waxed paper and roll out until very thin – about one-eighth of an inch. (It should not be so thin that it is see-through, but fondant is best eaten in smaller quantities. I personally like to use it like a

MEANWHILE...

BMO IS CUPCAKE!

BIDOOF!

HEY, I FOUND HIM!

sugary 'tortilla chip' to scoop frosting into my mouth. Don't judge, adventurer, I'm just being efficient.)

Roll out any other colors onto separate pieces of waxed paper and allow to dry to the touch on one side. This usually takes about an hour or so, depending on the humidity where you are.

Peel the fondant off the waxed paper and flip over, allowing the other side to dry as well, again for about another hour. (I did mention that you should make these ahead of time, right?)

While all this thrilling drying time is taking place, let's prep the templates: Print your desired template in black and white on regular printer paper. The template will be separated out into all its required pieces with each piece marked with what color it should be. For my example, there is one oval marked "yellow", and one bat shape marked "black." Cut shapes out with scissors, being careful to stay within the lines.

Once fondant is dry on both sides, pick a color. (I will start with black.) Place a small dot of shortening on the back of the template piece. This will help the template stick to the fondant and not slide around while you are cutting it. Using an X-acto knife or sharp paring knife that also has a thin layer of shortening on it, carefully cut around the template. It takes a steady hand, but with some practice, you will get a nice crisp edge *(Figures 2 and 3).*

(Figure 2)

(Figure 3)

Peel fondant piece off waxed paper and allow to dry overnight. If you are feeling thrifty, you can pop the leftover dried fondant into the microwave to soften, then re-knead into a soft ball. Store in plastic wrap in an airtight container until you need the color again in the future.

Finish cutting any remaining fondant sheets using the corresponding color template pieces. When all pieces are cut, allow to sit out overnight or for eight hours in a cool dry place.

When all pieces are completely dry, begin assembling them to match their completed photo example. Use a small brush to brush backs with water and press pieces together until affixed. You can also use a tiny amount of corn syrup or honey to affix the pieces to each other if you have it *(Figure 4)*.

Allow assembled toppers to dry another hour or two before placing them on top of your baked item of choice *(Figure 5)*. If toppers are going on top of a cupcake, press them down into the frosting at an angle to hold them in place.

(Figure 4)

(Figure 5)

Toppers can also be written on with edible ink markers, brushed with water followed by luster dust or disco dust / non-toxic glitter, or decorated with sprinkles. The sky's the limit! Experiment with your favorite baking supplies and see what you can come up with.

SKILL CHECK:

Some people will tell you to use gum paste here as it will set harder and last longer before wilting on the cupcakes. Those people are Demogorgons in disguise, because eating gum paste is more unpleasant than licking a Tiefling's undercarriage. Trust, adventurer, it is better to just limit the time the topper is on the cupcake by putting it on close to when they are going to be served than to subject your fellow adventurers to gum paste. Ugh.

A PARTY OF THRONES

You've done it, Dragon Slayer – your training is complete. But it looks like you've got one more challenge before you can rest. If the whispers are to be believed, an icy undead army is headed our way and winter is upon us… so we better throw one last party before the final battle begins!

Visit books.geeksweets.net to print your own 'Party of Thrones' invites!

— LEVEL 3 —
DRAGON SLAYER

QUEST REQUIREMENTS:

Red Velvet Cupcakes recipe
(see page 46)

Cream Cheese Frosting recipe
(see page 64)

Caramel or Dulce de Leche
ice cream topping

Graham Cracker crumbs
(or crushed graham crackers)

1 can cherry pie filling

2 small tubes red decorating gel

5-inch ball red fondant
(pre-dyed recommended)

Black gel food coloring
(and no-taste red if not using
pre-dyed red fondant)

Cupcake corer (optional)

Piping bag fitted with large round tip

Medium soft paintbrush

Toothpicks

Cupcake liners (red recommended)

DOTHRAKI HORSE HEART CUPCAKES

The room is silent as you stand in the center of those you wish to rule, with their eyes narrowed in distrust. Hold your horse heart cupcake aloft and proclaim your right to all in attendance – You are Daenerys Stormborn of the House Targaryen, First of Her Name, the Unburnt, Queen of the Andals and the First Men, Khaleesi of the Great Grass Sea. Eater of cupcakes! Om nom nom nooommm!

MAKES **22-24 CUPCAKES**

Preheat oven to 350° F; line cupcake tins with cupcake liners.

Create heart toppers: These toppers do not need to be made too far ahead of time, as they will not need to dry before placing them on the cupcakes.

Wearing gloves to protect your hands, dye vanilla fondant with no-taste red dye until a dark red color is achieved. If you have fondant that is already dyed, skip ahead to the next step, you keener.

Separate red fondant out into balls about 1 ½ inches wide, creating one for each cupcake you'll be baking. Shape balls into a cone shape with rounded edges *(Figure 1)*.

Create shapes to attach to the heart shape (ventricles, tube thingies… you know, heart stuff). Attach with a dot of water *(Figures 2 and 3)*.

(Figure 1)

(Figure 2)

(Figure 3)

(Figure 4)

With a toothpick, trace veins into heart shape, making sure they are deep so that they will show through the decorating gel that we'll be adding in a later step *(Figure 4)*. Set aside.

Prepare the Red Velvet Cupcakes recipe (see page 46).

Fill cupcake liners two-thirds of the way to the top with a disher or spoon. Bake 20 minutes, until a wooden toothpick inserted into the center of the cupcake comes out clean. Carefully remove from the cupcake pan and allow to come to room temperature.

When cupcakes are cooled, use a knife or a cupcake corer to remove a small amount of cake from the center of the cupcake. Feel free to nom immediately, or put in a ziplock bag in the freezer for future cake pops. (See page 52.)

Using a spoon, fill the cupcakes with cherry pie filling, making sure to get a few cherries in each one for maximum 'gore factor' when the cupcake is bitten into.

Prepare the Cream Cheese Frosting recipe (see page 64), mixing in 3-4 spoonfuls of the caramel ice cream topping. Taste test after mixing in the caramel and add more to taste. (If the topping is very thin, be careful not to add too much, as it will make the frosting too runny.)

Fill piping bag and frost cupcakes with a flat top, using a large round tip *(Figure 2)*. See page 28 for frosting techniques.

Pour about a cup of graham cracker crumbs into a small bowl, and press the top of the cupcake into them to cover the frosting. This will lay a 'sandy' base for the horse heart topper. Use the crushed up cookie crumbs to shape the frosting into a nice dome, dipping the sides first, then the top *(Figures 6, 7 and 8)*.

(Figure 5)

(Figure 6)

(Figure 7)

(Figure 8)

Using a medium-sized clean paintbrush (or your fingers!) smear some of the red gel onto the fondant hearts then sit them on top of the cupcake. Add a bit more gel dye so it drips down onto the 'sand'.

SKILL CHECK:

Better brush up on your Dothraki for your cupcake eating war-cry.
"Khalakka dothrae mr'anha!"

QUEST REQUIREMENTS:

2 ounces Midori

1 ounce vodka

2 ounces pineapple juice

3 ounces tonic water

Ice

Green glowing ice cube or glow stick (optional)

Cocktail shaker (or large mason jar or container for mixing)

SKILL CHECK:

For an extra dramatic presentation, (though not as dramatic as Cersei Lannister's Wildfire lightshow,) use a green glowstick bracelet as a stir stick. Also, the quinine in the tonic water will make the cocktail glow under black light - yay science!

WILDFIRE COCKTAIL

It may be the flammable result of years of malice, birthed into being by alchemists mad with power, but this potent green elixir sure packs a pleasing punch in a cocktail.

MAKES **1 VOLATILE COCKTAIL**

Shake Midori, vodka, pineapple juice and tonic water with ice in a cocktail shaker. Strain into a chilled cocktail glass with optional glowing green ice cube or glow stick in the bottom.

For a non-alcoholic version, replace Vodka and Midori with a tablespoon of green lime jello powder dissolved in a small amount of warm water, and increase tonic water and pineapple juice amounts to taste.

FESTIVAL REVELLER

"Your quest is complete! Celebrate the season with a glass of mead and these legendary seasonal recipes."

QUEST REQUIREMENTS:

No-Fail Sugar Cookie recipe (see page 72) or chocolate sugar cookie recipe (see page 74)

Royal Icing recipe (see page 70)

Gel food coloring (black, brown, teal, pink, orange, green, purple, yellow, and red)

White sprinkles (nonpareils)

Unvalentine Cookie template

Waxed paper

Rolling pin

Clean X-acto knife or sharp paring knife

3 piping bags fitted with #1 tips in black, teal, and red

6 piping bags fitted with #2 tips in white, pink, yellow, green, orange, and purple

Medium soft paintbrush

UNVALENTINE COOKIES

Pshhht, Valentine's Day. Who's got time for that when there's questing to be done? Share the "Meh" with these delish but dismissive sugar cookies, featuring the internet's grumpiest of cats.

MAKES **4-5 DOZEN HEARTS AND PISSED OFF KITTIES**

Prepare the No-Fail Sugar Cookie recipe from page 72, or the Chocolate Sugar Cookie recipe from page 74 if you're feeling chocolatey, to the point when dough is ready to roll out.

Roll out dough and cut into cat and heart shapes from the Unvalentine Cookie template and the instructions on page 35. (Visit books.geeksweets.net to print templates.)

Bake cookies at 350° F for 8-10 minutes or until just beginning to turn brown around the edges.

Prepare Royal Icing recipe from page 70 while cookies are cooling. Using the gel food coloring, make one-quarter cup of the icing black and another quarter cup teal for the eyes, then divide the remaining frosting into seven equal portions for the remaining colors (one portion will remain white). Fill piping bags as listed, following the directions on page 27.

While cookies are cooling, create grumpy eyes out of royal icing:

For the eyes, print the second page of the Unvalentine Cookie template in black and white. Lay out your printed templates with a piece of waxed paper over top, waxy side up. Use tape to hold both in place.

First outline the eyes in black with the #1 tip. Once dry, fill in the teal middles and add a single white sprinkle to the top left corner of the pupils. Make a few more than you will need in case they break when lifting them off the waxed paper. Allow to dry completely before peeling away from waxed paper *(Figures 1 to 6).*

(Figure 1)

(Figure 2)

(Figure 3)

(Figure 4)

(Figure 5)

(Figure 6)

Frost heart cookies: Frost one cookie at a time with pink, yellow, green, orange, and purple royal icing, using the "dam and flood" frosting technique from page 36. Allow to dry completely, about one hour, or until a crust has formed on top of the royal icing.

Frost cat cookies: Frost one cookie at a time with white royal icing, using the "dam and flood" cookie frosting technique from page 36 Allow to dry completely; allow at least two hours for drying, as we will be painting on them with a paintbrush in the next steps.

Pipe words onto the heart cookies: Using the piping bag filled with red royal icing and fitted with a #1 tip, pipe words on the "conversation heart" cookies *(Figures 7 and 8)*. They can be as grumpy or as non-grumpy as you like!

(Figure 7)

(Figure 8)

Mix up the edible "watercolor": Using a soft medium paintbrush and a small bowl or plate, mix up a small amount of the brown gel paste and water to create a watercolor for painting on the cat ears and whiskers. Mix up a second dot of brown with a little black in it to create a darker brown as well *(Figures 9 and 10)*.

(Figure 9)

(Figure 10)

Paint the ears and whiskers: using light strokes with a very small amount of the edible watercolor on your brush, paint the inside of the ears, and the whiskers behind where the eyes will be placed. Start in the middle of the cookie, and brush outward to the right and left sides, making two circles that join in the middle *(Figure 11)*. Using the darker color, outline the ears, and add a few strokes to the whiskers to add some texture *(Figure 12)*. Allow to dry.

(Figure 11)   *(Figure 12)*

Using a small dot of black royal icing, attach eyes. Pipe a pink triangle for nose and allow to dry. Once nose is dry, pipe upside down 'U' for mouth.

Allow cookies to completely dry overnight, then store in a sealed container at room temperature between pieces of waxed paper. Cookies can also be frozen for up to one month.

SKILL CHECK:

What follows is a list of possible phrases for your Unvalentine cookies which will properly portray your overall disdain for the holiday and all the mushy whatnot for which it stands: NO, GRUMP, BOO!, U SUCK, BITE ME, MEH, DISLIKE, SWIPE LEFT, DON'T TEXT, BAH!, PASS and HARD NO. Try piping some test words onto a piece of paper first to get used to the space required before piping the words on your cookies.

QUEST REQUIREMENTS:

*Moist Chocolate Cupcake recipe
(see page 44)*

*Classic Buttercream recipe
(see page 58)*

1 tablespoon vanilla

Gel food coloring (golden yellow)

Mini Cadbury Creme Eggs

For Creme Filling:

½ cup light corn syrup

¼ cup butter

1 teaspoon vanilla

¼ teaspoon salt

3 cups icing sugar, sifted

*5 piping bags, 4 intact, one fitted
with a medium round tip*

*Cupcake liners
(brown or black recommended)*

Cupcake corer (optional)

SKILL CHECK:

*To get the color of the inner creme
egg and frosting right on the money
for the classic Cadbury treat, use
Wilton's "golden yellow" gel food
coloring. If all you have is regular
yellow, mix a tiny amount of red in
with it to achieve the warmer shade.*

CREME EGG CUPCAKES

*A cupcake remake of the classic ooey, gooey Easter
basket favorite, these are best served sliced down the
middle to show off their impressive two-tone filling.*

MAKES **30-32 CUPCAKES**

Preheat oven to 350° F; line cupcake tins with cupcake liners.

Create the creme filling: With a stand or hand mixer,
mix together corn syrup, butter, vanilla, and salt in a large
bowl. Add icing sugar, one cup at a time, mixing slowly to
incorporate, then on medium-high speed until creamy.

Remove one-third of the creme filling mixture and place in
a small bowl. Add in golden yellow food coloring in small
amounts until mixture is a bright yellow color.

Add yellow-tinted creme filling to one piping bag, and
the remaining white creme filling to another. Tie ends with
elastics and set aside at room temperature *(Figures 1 and 2).*

(Figure 1)   *(Figure 2)*

Prepare the Moist Chocolate Cupcake recipe (see page 44).

Fill cupcake liners two-thirds of the way to the top with
a disher or spoon. Bake 15-20 minutes, until a wooden
toothpick inserted into the center of the cupcake comes out
clean. Carefully remove from the cupcake pan and allow to
come to room temperature.

When cupcakes are cooled, use a knife or a cupcake corer
to remove a small amount of cake from the center of the
cupcake. Cut the top off the removed bit of cupcake and

reserve *(Figures 3 and 4)*. Feel free to nom bottom half immediately, or put in a ziplock bag in the freezer for future cake pops. (See page 52.)

(Figure 3)

SAVE
THIS

NOM
THIS

(Figure 4)

Time for some tasty creme egg filling! Cut the tips off both of your piping bags filled with creme filling. First, fill the hole in a cupcake two-thirds of the way full with the white creme filling *(Figure 5)*. Next, take the tip of the yellow piping bag and press it down into the middle of the white creme filling in the cupcake. Squeeze until the hole in the cupcake is completely full *(Figure 6)*. Re-cap with the reserved bit of cupcake from step 7.

(Figure 5)

(Figure 6)

Prepare the Classic Buttercream recipe (see page 58), with one tablespoon of vanilla. Remove half of the buttercream from the mixing bowl. Dye the remaining buttercream yellow, and create a 2-color piping bag with the directions from page 33.

When cupcakes are cooled, frost a tall coil with 2-color buttercream using a medium round tip, (see page 28 for frosting techniques). Top with a mini Cadbury creme egg.

FESTIVAL REVELLER

QUEST REQUIREMENTS:

*No-Fail Sugar Cookie recipe
(see page 72)*

*3 tablespoons of your mom's
favorite tea, ground (Red Rose
Orange Pekoe for mine!)*

Royal Icing recipe (see page 70)

*Gel food coloring (brown for the
tea and your choice of color for the
china – I used magenta and teal)*

Mother's Day Tea Cookie template

Waxed paper

Rolling pin

*Clean X-acto knife or sharp
paring knife*

*2 piping bags fitted with #1 tips in
white and light brown*

*1 piping bag fitted with a #2 tip in
your chosen china color*

Small soft paintbrush

MOTHER'S DAY TEA COOKIES

*You may be ankle-deep in undead wurms, but you
ALWAYS make time for your momma, adventurer.
No exceptions.*

MAKES **4-5 DOZEN CUPS AND TEAPOTS**

Prepare the No-Fail Sugar Cookie recipe from page 72, adding in the three tablespoons of your chosen tea, finely ground, to the dry ingredients, up to the point when dough is ready to roll out.

Roll out dough and cut into teapot and teacup shapes using Mother's Day Tea Cookie template and the cookie dough rolling / cutting instructions from page 35. (Visit books.geeksweets.net to print template.) A cookie-cutter set can also be found listed in the Resources section of this book on page 259.

Bake cookies at 350° F for 8-10 minutes or until just beginning to turn brown around the edges. Carefully remove from baking sheet and allow to cool completely.

Prepare Royal Icing recipe from page 70 while cookies are cooling. Reserve a half cup of frosting to stay white. Using a very tiny amount of brown gel food coloring, tint another half cup until it is the shade of a cup of tea. Lastly, using the gel food coloring of your choice, tint the remaining royal icing. Fill piping bags as listed in the Quest Requirements, following the directions on page 27 for how to fill a piping bag.

Frost cookies: Frost one cookie at a time with royal icing in a color of your choice, using cookie frosting technique from page 36 *(Figure 1)*. Remember to leave an opening in the teacup to fill with tea. Allow to dry completely, at least two hours, as we will be painting on them with a paintbrush in the next steps.

Once dry, "fill the teacup" with tea from your light brown tinted piping bag. Optionally, you can also pipe an outline on the teapot lids, spouts, and teacup handles as well as outlining the poured tea in the teacup *(Figure 2)*.

(Figure 1)

(Figure 2)

One cookie at a time, pipe on the floral china pattern as shown in the template using the white royal icing. You can follow the pattern suggestion, or experiment with your own. Have elements of the pattern go off the edge of the cookie for a more 'natural placement' that looks as though it continues on the other side of the cookie *(Figure 3)*. Remember – only one cookie at a time! The icing will still need to be wet for the next step.

While the icing is still wet, use a small paintbrush to drag the line of frosting inward on the leaves and petals. *(Figure 4).* Use a light hand and work quickly so frosting does not dry out. Try to drag from the middle of the line down, not wipe away the line completely. Clean off your brush with a wet paper towel as you start to get a crusty build-up on your brush. Complete remaining cookies.

(Figure 3)

(Figure 4)

Starting with the cookies that are now dry, pipe a thin white line up the middle of the leaves, and small dots where the middle of the flowers would be. Also pipe small dots wherever there is a logical gap in the pattern, or where the pattern is looking a little sparse *(Figures 5 and 6).*

(Figure 5)

(Figure 6)

Allow cookies to dry completely overnight, then store in a sealed container at room temperature between pieces of waxed paper. Cookies can also be frozen for up to one month.

SKILL CHECK:

Tea can be ground in a variety of ways: with a coffee grinder, food processor, or a mortar and pestle, or else just chopped up finely with a knife. Depending on your variety of tea, it may already be fine enough as it is inside the tea bag. Generally we're just looking to avoid any big "tea chunks" or full leaves when eating the cookies.

QUEST REQUIREMENTS:

½ cup finely chopped pecans

3 tablespoons granulated sugar

1 box yellow cake mix

1 cup canned pumpkin
(not pumpkin pie mix)

½ cup water

1/3 cup vegetable oil

4 eggs

2 teaspoons pumpkin pie spice mix
(or ½ teaspoon each cinnamon,
ginger, nutmeg and allspice.)

**For Whipped Cream
Cheese Frosting:**

4 ounces cream cheese,
room temperature

¾ cup icing sugar

2 cups heavy / whipping
cream (36%)

Gold sparkling sugar sprinkles

QUEST REQUIREMENTS
CONTINUED ON PAGE 232

PUMPKIN PIE CUPCAKES

The big taste of pumpkin pie, transmogrified into cupcake
form, complete with pie crust and whipping cream!

MAKES **22-24 PUMPKIN PIES IN DISGUISE**

Preheat oven to 350° F; line cupcake tins with cupcake liners.

With a stand or hand mixer, beat cake mix, canned pumpkin,
water, oil, eggs, and pumpkin pie spices on low speed for 30
seconds, then on medium speed for two minutes, scraping
down the sides of the bowl occasionally with a spatula.

Fill cupcake liners two-thirds of the way to the top with
a disher or spoon. Bake 20-25 minutes, until a wooden
toothpick inserted into the center of the cupcake comes out
clean. Carefully remove from the cupcake pan and allow to
come to room temperature.

**While cupcakes are cooling, prepare the pie crust fall
leaf toppers:** Roll out pie crusts and cut 24 fall leaf shapes
from it, using the Pumpkin Pie Cupcake template *(Figures 1
and 2)*. Visit books.geeksweets.net to print template.

(Figure 1)   *(Figure 2)*

Arrange leaves on a parchment or silicone-lined baking
sheet. Using a pastry brush or your finger, brush each leaf
with a light coating of milk, and sprinkle generously with
sparkling sugar sprinkles, pressing down on sprinkles gently
with the back of a glass to help embed them into the
surface *(Figures 3 and 4)*. Bake until deep golden brown, 10 to
15 minutes. Let cool completely.

For Fall Leaf Toppers:

Rolled pie crust (store-bought, or homemade if you're feeling fancy)

¼ cup milk

White sparkling sugar sprinkles

Pumpkin Pie Cupcake template

Small paring knife or X-acto knife

1 piping bag fitted with large round tip

Cupcake liners (orange or brown recommended)

(Figure 3)

(Figure 4)

While leaves are cooling, prepare the Whipped Cream Cheese Frosting: With a stand or hand mixer, beat the cream cheese and icing sugar together until smooth. Add one cup of the cream and beat until soft peaks form. Add the remaining cup of cream, and beat until stiff peaks form. Stiff peaks are when you lift out the beater and the cream on the end of it comes to a point without folding over on itself. (It will take a while before it becomes stiff enough to pipe – a stand mixer with a whisk attachment is recommended, but a hand mixer and some of that strong-willed adventurer spirit should do the trick as well!) Transfer the mixture to a piping bag fitted with a large round tip.

Frost cupcakes with a **flat top** (see page 28 for frosting techniques), and top with fall leaf toppers and a sprinkling of sparkling sugar sprinkles.

QUEST REQUIREMENTS:

For Sugar Glass:

2 cups water

1 cup light (not golden) corn syrup

3 ½ cups granulated sugar

¼ teaspoon cream of tartar

Red Velvet Cupcakes recipe (see page 46)

Cream Cheese Frosting recipe (see page 64)

Red decorating gel

Clean baking sheet, 13" x 18" or close to that size

Piping bag fitted with large round tip

Cupcake liners (silver, black, or white recommended)

BROKEN GLASS CUPCAKES

Sharp! To avoid any trip-ups making the glass, it's best to use a candy thermometer. The sugar should be cooked on low – cooking it too fast or too hot will cause it to caramelize too quickly. I start on low and ramp it up to nearly medium over the course of an hour, and my glass comes out nice and clear. It's a time commitment, but you just can't rush sugar, adventurer.

MAKES **22-24 CUPCAKES**

Make the sugar glass: Combine water, light corn syrup, sugar, and cream of tartar in a large saucepan and bring to a boil on medium-low heat. Using a candy thermometer, continue to boil sugar syrup on medium low until temperature reaches 300° (or the "hard crack" stage), stirring constantly. The mixture will thicken as the water evaporates *(Figure 1)*.

Patience is required here, adventurer, as it will take a good long time to get there, but once it reaches 300° (the 'hard crack' stage, just before the mixture starts to brown), quickly pour it onto a clean metal baking pan. Beware – pan will be very hot! Wearing oven mitts, quickly pick up pan and tilt from side to side until sugar has spread from corner to corner in a thin layer *(Figure 2)*. Set aside to cool completely.

(Figure 1)

(Figure 2)

Preheat oven to 350° F; line cupcake tins with cupcake liners.

Prepare the Red Velvet Cupcakes recipe (see page 46).

Fill cupcake liners two-thirds of the way to the top with a disher or spoon. Bake 20 minutes, until a wooden toothpick

---

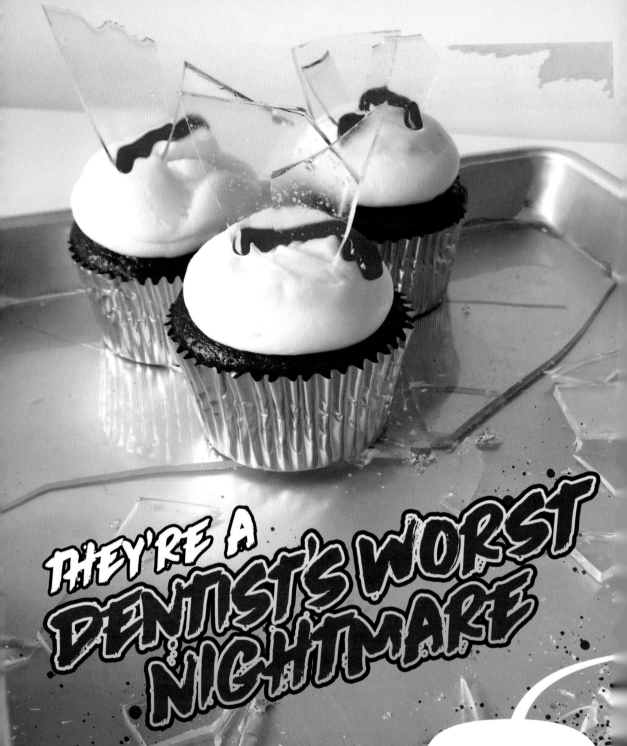

inserted into the center of the cupcake comes out clean. Carefully remove from the cupcake pan and allow to come to room temperature.

While cupcakes are cooling, prepare the Cream Cheese Frosting recipe (see page 64).

Fill piping bag and frost a flat top on the cupcakes with large round tip (see page 28 for frosting techniques).

Time for the best part – smashing! By now, Dragon Slayer, I estimate that you are an expert at smashing. Grab the sheet of cooled sugar glass, and using a meat mallet or battle axe, tap the surface of the glass until it shatters. Break it in about 4 places, evenly spaced *(Figures 3 and 4)*. Don't go too crazy, or your pieces will be too tiny!

(Figure 3)

(Figure 4)

Carefully pick shards of glass from the baking sheet and stick them into the cupcakes, deep enough so they will stay put. I like to put two or three pieces of varying sizes on top of each cupcake. Use the red decorating gel to pipe some blood drips where the glass pierces the frosting. One small tube will do about 24 'moderately bloodied' cupcakes, so don't use it all up at the beginning - you can always go back and add more blood as desired.

SKILL CHECK:

Can't get your hands on a candy thermometer? Then grab a glass of cold water and we'll do it the old-fashioned way. Drop a little of the molten syrup from a spoon into the water and it should form hard, brittle threads that break when bent. This is the 'hard crack' stage. If the consistency is anything less rigid than that, for example, something resembling salt-water taffy or nougat when squished between your fingers, then you're not quite there yet.

SKILL CHECK:

The red gel will eventually start to solidify in a strange, gummy fashion, so it's recommended that you put the gel on close to when you are serving these bad boys.

EYEBALL CAKE POPS

These gross, gory pops are popular around All Hallow's Eve with the younglings. What is it with younglings and a fascination with disembodied parts? Little necromancers in the making, they are.

MAKES **40-50 CREEPY PEEPERS**

Follow cake pop recipe from page 52, right up until the pops are ready to attach to sticks.

Place a cake ball on a flat surface. Using a single candy melt wafer, press an indentation into the cake ball, giving it one flat side. Once dipped, this is the spot where we will attach the "iris." Repeat with all remaining cake balls *(Figures 1 and 2).*

(Figure 1)

(Figure 2)

Melt white candy melts as directed in the cake pop recipe on page 52. Instead of using a lollipop stick, dip the first half inch of a plastic fork into the melted candy melts and attach to the bottom of the eyeball shape by pushing pop halfway down onto the fork *(Figures 3 and 4)*. The bottom of the eyeball is the part that was sitting on the table in the last step, and the flat indentation made in the pop by the candy melt should be facing forward.

(Figure 3)

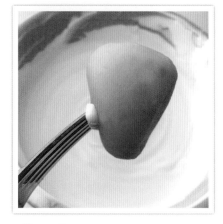

(Figure 4)

While the pops are drying, take a paper towel and wipe off the surface of the candy melts you will be using as irises. They will usually have an uneven, waxy surface from bumping into each other in the bag, and a quick wipe-down will help even them out *(Figures 5 and 6)*.

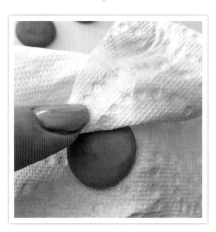

(Figure 5)

(Figure 6)

Once all pops are on forks, it's time to start dipping. If your bowl of white candy melts is starting to harden on the edges, re-melt in the microwave in 30 second intervals until thin enough for dipping.

Holding pop upside down, dip into candy melts until completely submerged. Be sure none of the cake ball is showing between the fork prongs, as we will need a tight seal of chocolate around the cake to avoid any oil seeping out of the pop. Tap fork on side of bowl to drip off excess chocolate *(Figure 7)*. While the chocolate is still wet, press a red, blue, or green "iris" into the flat indentation we left in the front of the pop in step 2 *(Figure 8)*.

(Figure 7)

(Figure 8)

Sit pop in styrofoam block to dry. Repeat with remaining pops until you have 50 pupil-less dead eyeballs staring back at you.

Once pops are dry, use a black edible ink pen to draw a round pupil in the middle of the colored candy melt "iris". The smaller the pupil you draw, the more manic the eyeball will look *(Figure 9)*.

Attach a small white sprinkle to the top right-hand corner of the pupil with a tiny bit of candy melt, dotted on with the back of a toothpick *(Figure 10)*. If you don't have sprinkles, you can just use a larger dot of white candy melt applied with a toothpick.

(Figure 9)

(Figure 10)

Using the red decorating gel, pipe two or three drops of blood coming from the base of the cake pop, where it attaches to the fork. Allow to dry for an hour before serving. Pops can be stored at room temperature in a cool dry place for up to a week from the day the original cake was baked.

QUEST REQUIREMENTS:

*Foolproof Vanilla Cupcakes recipe
(see page 42)*

*Classic Buttercream recipe
(see page 58)*

1 can cherry pie filling

*Gel food coloring (no-taste red
and black)*

*1 piping bag fitted with a small
round tip (Ateco 802)*

*Cupcake liners
(white recommended)*

SKILL CHECK:

*Serve cupcakes with napkins! Those
gooey brain innards can come as
a surprise, and the mage tower
carpeting might never recover.*

BRAIN CUPCAKES

*Town overrun by undead looking to score some juicy
human brains? No problem – swap in some of these cherry-
filled counterparts in place of actual human grey matter.
Zombies aren't known for their high perception stat.*

MAKES **22-25 CUPCAKES**

Preheat oven to 350° F; line cupcake tins with cupcake liners.

Prepare the Foolproof Vanilla Cupcakes recipe (see page 42).

Fill cupcake liners two-thirds of the way to the top with
a disher or spoon. Bake 15 - 20 minutes, until a wooden
toothpick inserted into the center of the cupcake comes out
clean. Carefully remove from the cupcake pan and allow to
come to room temperature.

While cupcakes are cooling, prepare the Classic Buttercream
recipe (see page 58).

Tint buttercream with a tiny amount of no-taste red gel food
coloring by adding coloring to buttercream with a toothpick.
(No double dipping!) Once you have a very light pink, mix
in an even tinier amount of black to point the pink in a more
"grey matter" direction. Mix to completely incorporate color.

When cupcakes are cooled, use a knife or a cupcake corer
to remove a small amount of cake from the center of the
cupcake. Feel free to nom immediately, or put in a ziplock
bag in the freezer for future cake pops. (See page 52.)

(Figure 1)

Using a spoon, fill the
cupcakes with cherry pie
filling, making sure to get a
few cherries in each one for
maximum "gore factor" when
the cupcake is bitten into
(Figure 1).

Frost cupcakes: In the piping
bag fitted with a small round
tip (with a hole about double
the diameter of a pencil),

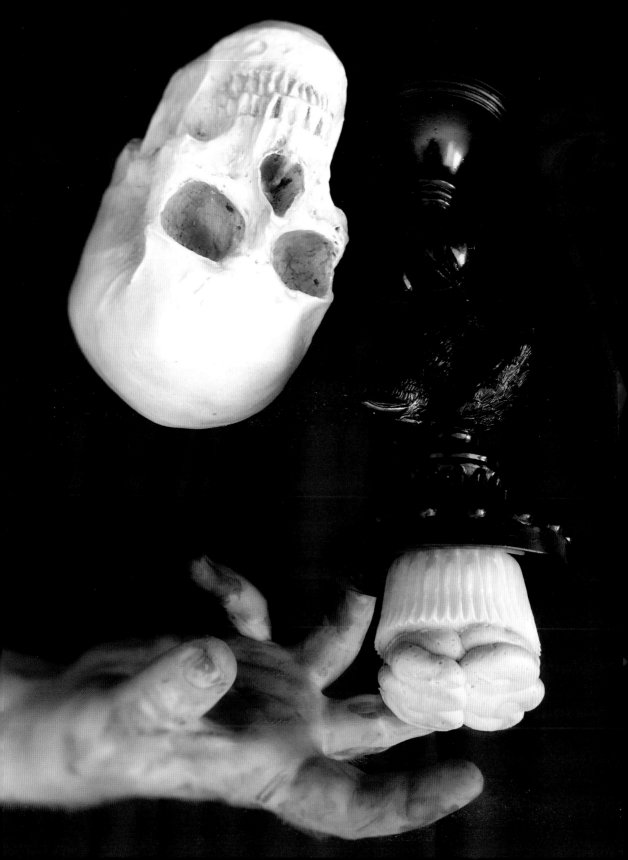

pipe a backwards capital 'D' and a second forward facing capital 'D', back to back as pictured *(Figures 2 and 3)*.

(Figure 2)

(Figure 3)

Using a zigzag motion with rounded corners, pipe one side of the cupcake, then the other, covering the 'D's' created in the last step. Try to match the zigzags so the two sides are mirrored *(Figures 4 and 5)*.

(Figure 4)

(Figure 5)

FESTIVAL REVELLER

QUEST REQUIREMENTS:

For the Cupcakes:

1 ½ cups all-purpose flour

2 tablespoons ground ginger

2 teaspoons ground cinnamon

¼ teaspoon ground cloves

¼ teaspoon ground nutmeg

1 ½ cups butter, room temperature

1 ½ cups granulated sugar

3 tablespoons molasses

4 eggs

1 teaspoon vanilla

For the Lil' Gingerbread Fella Cookie Toppers:

½ cup salted butter

¼ cup packed brown sugar

2 ½ cups all-purpose flour

½ teaspoon baking powder

¼ teaspoon salt

1 ½ teaspoons ground cinnamon

1 ½ teaspoons ground ginger

½ teaspoons ground cloves

1 egg

½ cup molasses

Black edible ink pen

Gold luster dust

QUEST REQUIREMENTS
CONTINUED ON PAGE 238

GINGERBREAD CUPCAKES

"Run, run, as fast as you can, you'll never catch me, I'm the gingerbread man!"

Clearly this gingerbread man has never heard of your Blood-Forged Footguards of Agility.

MAKES **20-22 CUPCAKES**

Preheat oven to 350° F, line cupcake tins with cupcake liners.

Make lil' gingerbread fellas: With a stand or hand mixer, cream butter and brown sugar on medium speed until light and fluffy, about three minutes. Add egg and molasses, scraping the sides cf the bowl with a spatula as needed. Reduce speed to low.

Mix together flour, salt, baking powder, and spices with a whisk and slowly add to bowl with creamed butter mixture. Mix until combined.

Roll out dough and cut into lil' gingerbread fellas using the Gingerbread Cupcakes template and instructions on page 35, and the dough-rolling instructions on page 34. (If you have a small gingerbread cookie cutter in your arsenal, feel free to go ahead and use it instead, otherwise visit books. geeksweets.net to print template.)

(Figure 1)

Bake cookies at 350° F for 12-14 minutes or until just beginning to turn brown around the edges (Figure 1). Allow to cool completely. Once cool, use an edible ink pen to draw eyes and mouth, and a little gold luster dust mixed with a tiny amount of vodka to dot on his two buttons (Figures 2 and 3). See page 39 for how to paint tiny luster dust details.

QUEST REQUIREMENTS:

For the Cinnamon Cream Cheese frosting:

Cream Cheese Frosting recipe (see page 64)

1 teaspoon cinnamon

1 teaspoon vanilla

Gingerbread Cupcakes template

Waxed paper

Rolling pin

Clean X-acto knife or sharp paring knife

1 piping bag fitted with a large star tip

Cupcake liners (brown recommended)

SKILL CHECK:

The lil' gingerbread fellas will soften as they sit on the frosting, so if you like your men crunchy (and who doesn't really), add to top of cupcakes shortly before serving.

(Figure 2)   (Figure 3)

Make gingerbread cupcakes: In a large bowl, mix together flour and spices with a whisk. Set aside.

In the bowl of a stand mixer fitted with a paddle attachment, cream butter and sugar until light and fluffy, about three minutes. Beat in the molasses until incorporated, followed by the eggs, one at a time. Add in vanilla.

Add flour and spice mixture and mix on low speed until combined. (Be careful not to overmix!)

Fill cupcake liners two-thirds of the way to the top with a disher or spoon. Bake 22-25 minutes, until a wooden toothpick inserted into the center of the cupcake comes out clean. Carefully remove from the cupcake pan and allow to come to room temperature.

While cupcakes are cooling, prepare the Cream Cheese Frosting recipe (see page 64). Add cinnamon and vanilla and beat until combined.

Fill piping bag and frost a **classic rosette** with large star tip (see page 28 for frosting techniques). Top with lil' gingerbread fella. Then eat him first!

FESTIVAL
REVELLER

QUEST REQUIREMENTS:

No-Fail Sugar Cookie recipe
(see page 72)

Royal Icing recipe (see page 70)

1 bag regular size marshmallows

Gel food coloring (black)

Orange candy-coated chocolate
chips (or orange candy of any
kind: sprinkles, Nerds candy, fuzzy
peaches, orange Starburst, etc.)

Assorted round and heart shaped
sprinkles in various colors

Gold and silver dragées

Melted Snowman Cookie template

Waxed paper

Rolling pin

Clean X-acto knife or
sharp paring knife

1 piping bag fitted with a #3 tip,
filled with white royal icing

1 piping bag fitted with a #1 tip,
filled with black royal icing

MELTED SNOWMAN COOKIES

*Not even the strongest of your arcane magics can keep
Frosty from thawing come spring. Life is beautiful but
fleeting, adventurer, always remember that.*

Now, time to feast on his remains!

MAKES **4-5 DOZEN SAD SNOWMEN**

Prepare the No-Fail Sugar Cookie recipe on page 72 as
directed to the point when dough is ready to roll out.

Roll out dough and cut into "melted snow blobs" using the
Melted Snowman Cookie template and the cookie dough
rolling / cutting instructions from page 35 *(Figure 1 and 2)*.
Visit books.geeksweets.net to print template. Feel free to
"just wing it" for the shapes, as they are just random puddle
shapes and don't need to be perfect – the template can
give you some shape ideas if you'd like to just go for it.

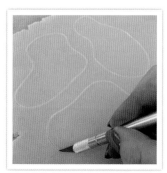

(Figure 1)

(Figure 2)

Bake cookies at 350° F for 8-10 minutes or until just
beginning to turn brown around the edges. Carefully
remove from baking sheet and allow to cool completely.

Prepare Royal Icing recipe from page 70 while cookies are
cooling. Remove all but three-quarters of a cup of frosting
and store in a sealed container, or a bowl covered with a wet
cloth. Set aside.

To the remaining three-fourths cup of royal icing, add black
gel dye until a nice dark shade of black is achieved.

Fill piping bags as listed in the Quest Requirements, following the directions on how to fill a piping bag on page 27.

Prepare snowman heads: using a small amount of margarine or butter on a piece of paper towel, grease the surface of a large dinner plate. Not too much – just a very thin layer to keep the marshmallows from sticking.

Place about five or six marshmallows on a plate spaced at least two inches apart, and heat in the microwave for 10-15 seconds, until the marshmallows begin to expand just slightly. Then remove from microwave and allow to deflate *(Figure 3)* . This will give them the droopy "I'm melting, I'm meeeeeelting!" vibe we're looking for.

Frost one cookie at a time with white royal icing, using the "dam and flood" cookie frosting technique from page 36. While frosting is still wet, carefully lift a partially melted marshmallow off the plate and press into the wet icing *(Figure 4)*. Complete with remaining cookies and allow to dry completely, at least two hours.

(Figure 3)

(Figure 4)

Using the black frosting in a piping bag fitted with a #1 tip, pipe stick arms and hands that start at the base of the marshmallow - see template for positioning examples. Pipe dots for mouths and eyes (or X's for eyes if you're feeling macabre).

Using dots of white icing, attach a small orange candy-coated chocolate chip or a piece of candy fashioned into a triangle for a nose, two heart sprinkles for a bowtie, and sprinkles or silver balls for buttons *(Figures 5 and 6)*.

(Figure 5)

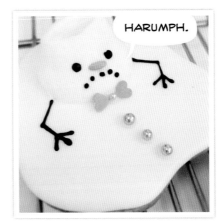

(Figure 6)

Allow cookies to dry completely overnight, then store in a sealed container at room temperature between pieces of waxed paper, no more than two rows high, or the marshmallows will start to smoosh. Cookies can also be frozen for up to one month.

THE ROCKING DEAD

This is the end of your journey, adventurer. You've bested all levels and branches of the baking skill tree and reveled in your success. Time to kick back, relax, and… wait a minute… what is that shambling in your direction? It's moaning and chomping and reaching out towards you. You stand up and reach back…

"Wait!" shouts a bearded man in a tattered looking sheriff's uniform. He takes off his hat and takes aim at what you can now see is an undead being, furiously grasping at you.

"I've got this," you say, as you reach for your +12 Axe of Undoing. A hero's work is never done, Dragon Slayer. Cue your theme music.

Visit books.geeksweets.net to print 'Rocking Dead' invites!

QUEST REQUIREMENTS:

No-Fail Sugar Cookie recipe
(see page 72)

Red decorating gel

Cocoa powder

Sliced almonds

Yellow gel food coloring (optional)

Soft large brush

Disher or ice cream scoop
(optional)

SKILL CHECK:

Optionally, you can toast the almonds for improved flavor and a bit more weathered look. You can also rub a very small amount of yellow gel food dye right at the base of the nail for maximum decomposition realness.

WALKER FINGER COOKIES

Keep them as a snack, or tie them around your neck like a certain crossbow-wielding heartthrob's ear necklace. Walker accessories are all the rage this apocalypse – who knew?

MAKES **8-10 DOZEN DIGITS**

Prepare the No-Fail Sugar Cookie recipe on page 72 as directed to the point when dough is complete.

Separate out dough into equal sized balls about two inches wide, using a disher or ice cream scoop. (You can also use a kitchen scale to make equal sized balls, or just eyeball them like a pro – you're a Dragon Slayer now, go for it!)

Roll balls out into finger shapes with a first and second knuckle. If you're in need of a reference, use the very fingers you're using to do the shaping! Exaggerate the knuckles for a more emaciated and gnarled zombie finger, and unevenly tear off the very end of the fingers where they would have attached to the hand *(Figure 1)*.

(Figure 1)   *(Figure 2)*

Using the blunt side of a kitchen knife, add in the curved wrinkles around the knuckles, again using your own fingers as a visual reference *(Figure 2)*.

Take a sliced almond and press it down into the fingertip to make an indentation in the cookie. Remove the almond, as you won't bake it in with the cookies. Instead, this indentation will make a spot to add it back into later *(Figure 3)*.

Bake cookies at 350° F for 8-10 minutes or until just beginning to turn brown around the edges. Remove from oven.

When cookies are cooled, brush on a small amount of cocoa powder for that "I just dug myself out of my own grave" look *(Figure 4)*.

(Figure 3)

(Figure 4)

While cookies are still warm, place a blob of red decorating gel in the indentation you made in step 5 *(Figure 5)*. Press a sliced almond into place, pointed side up, as the fingertip. Red gel will ooze out around the almond in a deliciously gruesome fashion *(Figure 5)*.

(Figure 5)

(Figure 6)

(Figure 7)

Let cookie [...] llow gel to set for a couple of hou[...] ver completely dry and will remain tacky, [...] ll set enough to keep the fingernails in p[...].) For an even more rotted look, paint a small amount of yellow gel dye at the base of the nail *(Figure 6)*.

QUEST REQUIREMENTS:

2 ounces rye or bourbon

3 dashes Angostura bitters

1 sugar cube (or ½ teaspoon of granulated sugar)

Club soda

Clear corn syrup (or honey)

Wilton silver granulated sugar

Red decorating gel

Ice

1 old fashioned glass (usually a short, heavy bottomed tumbler)

SKILL CHECK:

No Angostura bitters lying around in your potions cabinet? Mix a pinch of cinnamon, ground clove, and nutmeg with one-quarter teaspoon of lemon zest, one-quarter teaspoon of finely-diced prunes, and two tablespoons of vodka or rum.

LUCILLE COCKTAIL

Named after the barbed wire wrapped bat of the trash-talking villain you love to hate, and hate that you love so much. Uungh. I blame Jeffrey Dean Morgan.

MAKES **1 NEWFANGLED OLD FASHIONED**

Place the silver granulated sugar in a wide bowl.

Using your fingers, spread the clear corn syrup or honey around the rim of the glass and turn it upside down in the silver sugar crystals to create your spiky "barbed wire" rim *(Figures 1 and 2).*

(Figure 1)

(Figure 2)

Using the red decorating gel, trace a ring just under the sugar rim on the inside of the glass and allow to 'drip down' a bit into the glass *(Figure 3).*

(Figure 3)

Add two or three dashes of Angostura bitters and a quick splash (about a tablespoon) of club soda to the bottom of the glass. Mash the sugar and bitters together with a wooden muddler (or the handle of a wooden spoon), then rotate glass to spread the mash around the bottom.

Add a large ice cube, or 2-3 medium sized ones, and pour the rye or bourbon over it.

RESOURCES

Wandering merchants, witch doctors, and websites, for all your sweet spellcasting needs.

ThinkGeek

thinkgeek.com

In addition to being an awesome source of geek goodies, ThinkGeek has a sizable section of kitchen supplies. Cookie cutters, silicone molds, aprons, Star Wars spatulas... you'll have the geekiest kitchen in the land.

Golda's Kitchen

goldaskitchen.com

For Canadian wizards who want to save on shipping, Golda's has an amazing selection of baking supplies, and it is my go-to for baking cups. So very many baking cups.

WarpZone Prints

warpzoneprints.com

3D printed cookie cutters from all your favorite fandoms. And if you're looking for something super specific, they'll print you a custom cookie cutter from your own design. Neato!

India Tree

indiatree.com

Searched the realm high and low for the perfect sprinkle and came up with nothing? You can bet India Tree will have it. And as a bonus, many of their ingredients are made with natural flavors and colors.

Global Sugar Art

globalsugarart.com

An unending selection of baking supplies, including some harder to find items like tylose powder to thicken fondant, and gold and silver highlighter for making things shiny.

Michaels
michaels.com

Michaels is a craft store with an ever-growing baking aisle that gets more and more impressive every year. They have every Wilton product under the sun, and a huge selection of bakeware. Download their app and get a 40% off coupon for your giant box of fondant.

BulkBarn
bulkbarn.ca

Tips, flavoring, sanding sugars, sprinkles, candy melts, cookie cutters, candies, baking pans and more. Just don't let them catch you sneaking a jelly bean from the bins – they really frown on it. I mean, you should still do it. Just don't let them catch you.

WebstaurantStore
webstaurantstore.com

Ready to start baking for the geek masses? This online store has everything you'll need to start hawking your wizardly wares, like bakery cases, tiers, and disposable packaging.

Amazon
amazon.com

You may have heard of it, it's only the biggest, baddest, most multinational retail entity out there. When all else fails, they'll have it.

ABOUT THE AUTHOR

A graphic designer by day, Sweet Geek Jenny Burgesse found another passion buried beneath a pile of flour and dutch process cocoa powder. Geek Sweets began in Ottawa as a home-based bakery, with everything made from scratch, just like grandma used to make – If grandma made Cthulhu Cookies and Battlestar Galacticakes. After finding success on the great plains of The Internet, Jenny and her trusty sidekick Mr. B relocated to Vancouver to be close to family, to be a part of the Farmer's Market scene, and to continue their baking quest in the city that holds their hearts.